150 STORIES

Celebrating 150 Years of People, Places, and Events
That Defined Boston Conservatory

Boston Conservatory at Berklee

Boston, Massachusetts

150 Stories: Celebrating 150 Years of People, Places, and Events That Defined Boston Conservatory
Published by Boston Conservatory at Berklee
8 Fenway
Boston, Massachusetts 02215-4006

USA
First Printing
May 2017
Library of Congress Control Number: 2017937220
ISBN 978-0-9884026-1-4

Executive Editor: Andrea Di Cocco
Contributing Authors: Carol Beggy, Andrea Di Cocco, Samantha Burns, Richard Ortner, Roger H. Brown
Foreword: Jamie Bernstein
Cover Art: Alyssa Kerr
Art Director: Alyssa Kerr
Designer: Cia Boynton, Boynton Hue Studio
Editor: Susan Gedutis Lindsay
Researcher: Carol Beggy
Staff Archivist: Brendan Higgins
Production Supervisor: Samantha Burns
Printing: Reynolds-DeWalt Corporation

Dedication

This book is dedicated to the countless individuals—students, alumni, faculty, staff, administrators, parents, supporters, and community members—who have made Boston Conservatory an extraordinary and truly unique place to learn and grow. May the stories on these pages serve as reminder that the arts have the power to bring communities together and change the world.

Contents

The First Hundred Years: 1867–1966

Foreword

Jamie Bernstein

It's always an exciting moment when a celebration of the past reveals a path to the future. As Boston Conservatory turns a grand and venerable 150 years old, we can marvel at the way its very beginnings contained the DNA of all the innovation and visionary growth that followed, and that of which is still very much to come.

The vision began with the founder of Boston Conservatory, the extraordinary Julius Eichberg. Like all musicians of import in those days, Eichberg came from Europe—in this case, Germany. But Eichberg's work enabled American-born performing artists to one day be leaders in their fields and in their country.

Eichberg could have stayed in Europe and enjoyed a lucrative music career. At the age of 7, he had already been singled out for his prowess on the violin by no less than Czar Nicholas I of Russia, and he was later recommended to the Royal Conservatory in Brussels by Felix Mendelssohn himself. One could not have hoped for a more illustrious launch. His career as a concert violinist was assured, and his compositional efforts would most certainly have received attention and respect.

But instead, Eichberg came to the United States and settled in Boston, a small city that did not yet have its own music conservatory. And so, Eichberg started one in 1867, and Boston Conservatory of Music was born.

That very same year, Eichberg also became Boston's Supervisor of Music for the city's public schools. (Imagine if our city governments had such a position today!) Clearly, this was a man on fire about education. But his vision burned even brighter.

From the very first days of the Conservatory's existence, Eichberg made sure that women had equal access to his school's resources. The classrooms and rehearsal spaces at 154 Tremont Street were nearly as full of young women as they were of young men. He even launched Boston's first all-female professional string quartet, the Eichberg Quartet, comprised of Boston Conservatory students, and he made sure they got paid, too.

Eichberg went even further. He recruited talented musicians and instructors to his school, and it was through his efforts that African American musicians began training at Boston schools. These students included P.G. Lowery, a Kansas native who traveled to Boston to study at the Conservatory. Lowery, the first African American to receive his training at the Conservatory, went on to be a celebrated cornet player, circus bandleader, and close friend of Scott Joplin.

But even still, Eichberg was far from done. In 1873, he selected his operetta, *The Doctor of Alcantara,* to be performed by an African American cast. It was performed in Washington D.C. by the original Colored American Opera Company, the first African American opera company in the United States. At the time, all these efforts must have seemed somewhat unusual, coming from this German violinist; today, we can't help but be astonished by Eichberg's prescience and generosity of spirit.

These qualities of Eichberg's have persevered well beyond his lifetime. After Eichberg's death in 1893, his family allowed *The Doctor of Alcantara* to be used as a fundraising tool for Boston youth programs. Today, Boston public schools are fighting to bring back music within their walls; Julius Eichberg would be heartened to see that some progress is being made at last.

In his eulogy for Eichberg, Unitarian Reverend Minot J. Savage said of his late friend: "He loved all the sister arts; he counted them as one family." It was Eichberg's embrace of all the arts that, in the twentieth century, led to the expansion of Boston Conservatory to include its now-legendary departments of dance, opera, and theater. The first expansion came in the 1920s, with the addition of opera. Composition and drama were added in the 1930s. Then, in 1943, dance got a department, thereby turning the Boston Conservatory into the multifaceted institution it is today.

Expansion is still very much in the air. As Boston Conservatory contemplates its next 150 years, it has lost none of its visionary audacity. In fact, under the guidance of its visionary president, Richard Ortner, it launched into what is perhaps its grandest adventure of all: the merger of the Conservatory with Berklee.

In the Conservatory's ability to take these new leaps, we can discern those very elements—diversity, gender equality, and a passion for the teaching and learning of beauty—that Julius Eichberg put in place from the very beginning.

Happy 150th, Boston Conservatory—and onward you go!

Jamie Bernstein is a narrator, writer, and broadcaster who has transformed a lifetime of loving music into a career of sharing her knowledge and excitement with others. She is the daughter of esteemed American composer/conductor Leonard Bernstein.

Note to the Reader

Intent

When we set out to create this book, we intended it as a simple compilation of the stories that have defined Boston Conservatory over its 150-year history. But as we researched the school's people, places, and events, we uncovered fascinating details about the Conservatory that had never before been chronicled. And so, in the true spirit of the Conservatory, we adjusted our approach and set out to create what we believe to be the only complete account of the school's history over its first 150 years. We hope that *150 Stories* provides insight into Boston Conservatory's rich—and sometimes tumultuous—history, and helps illustrate the vision and perseverance that has always carried the institution into its next chapter.

Usage of the Name

Throughout this publication, readers will see many variations in how the Conservatory's official name appears. Given that the school's name has undergone a number of iterations throughout its history (detailed on the next page), we have attempted to honor the formal name of the institution as it was during the time period covered in the story. Therefore, some stories may refer to the school as "Boston Conservatory of Music," in the instance of an earlier era, while others may refer to the school as "The Boston Conservatory," in the instance of a more recent era. The editors have made every effort to ensure consistent and proper usage of the school's name per article.

The People

The people highlighted in this publication represent only a handful of the extraordinary individuals who have influenced the Conservatory over the years. In an effort to be inclusive of as many accounts as possible, the school reached out to community members and encouraged anyone with a defining Conservatory story to share it for the purpose of this publication. We received many recommendations, self-submissions, and referrals, and we have done our best to honor all voices. It should go without saying that despite our best efforts, there are still many more stories yet to be uncovered. We hope that *150 Stories* will be an ongoing project for Boston Conservatory, and we encourage everyone with additional information to share their stories with the school. Please note: Alumni degrees, areas of concentrations, and graduation years are indicated wherever the information is available. Because recordkeeping style varied over the history of the institution, academic information is not available for all alumni mentioned in this publication.

Acknowledgments

Boston Conservatory at Berklee graciously acknowledges the following people for their generous support to the Conservatory and help in making this book possible: Berklee Trustees and Leadership Council, Boston Conservatory at Berklee Board of Overseers, Richard Ortner, Roger H. Brown, David Scott Sloan, Anthony Pangaro, Gary Mikula, Alfred D. Houston, William Seymour, Tom Riley, and all members of the Berklee leadership who provided insight; Boston Conservatory students, faculty, staff, and alumni who submitted information for stories and provided a wealth of historical knowledge and memories, with special thanks to Conservatory Archivist Brendan Higgins for his unwavering attention to detail; Jamie Bernstein for sharing her passion for the arts and Boston's rich history; Boston author Carol Beggy for dedicating countless hours to researching, interviewing, and writing stories for this book; Annemarie Lewis Kerwin and Leslie Jacobson Kaye for getting this project off the ground; Samantha Burns for organizing and managing all phases of production; Susan Gedutis Lindsay and Cia Boynton for their professional expertise, guidance, and collaboration; and last, but not least, Julius Eichberg, whose vision inspired 150 years of passion, goodwill, and performing arts excellence.

Evolution of the School's Name

Artifacts and images featuring the various iterations of the name from 1867–2017

When **Julius Eichberg** founded **Boston Conservatory of Music** in the winter of 1867, the name was an accurate reflection the school's mission. Eichberg, a composer and renowned teacher of violin and strings, opened the Conservatory to offer his students a more formal conservatory-style education, rather than the "lessons" that most aspiring musicians came to receive at the time. In those first years, the Conservatory taught only music, with an almost exclusive focus on strings.

During the latter part of Eichberg's tenure, he scoured the region to find top teachers and musicians as a way to attract exceptional students from around the country to attend the Conservatory.

By that time, Eichberg's school had expanded its reach by training brass players, most notably on the cornet, and later piano and harpsichord.

When Eichberg died in 1893, **R. Marriner Floyd** took over the Conservatory's business operations, and **Herman P. Chelius** was appointed musical director. According to a report in *The Boston Sunday Post* newspaper of June 21, 1896, Floyd announced that the Conservatory had been reorganized as a corporation operating under the same name, **Boston Conservatory of Music**.

Nearly twenty years later, on August 15, 1914, Floyd filed the paperwork needed

to formally change the institution's name to **The Boston Conservatory and College of Oratory**. In a bit of a historic twist, when **Charles Wesley Emerson** founded his nearby school in 1880 as the Boston Conservatory of Elocution, Oratory, and Dramatic Art, there was understandable confusion between Emerson and Eichberg's schools, which—according to the news of the day—prompted calls for Emerson to change the name of his school. Emerson did that a year later when he renamed his new school the Monroe Conservatory of Oratory. It was later changed to Emerson College of Oratory, known today as Emerson College.

When the internationally recognized opera conductor **Agide Jacchia** took the helm of the Conservatory in 1920, the school's name legally included "and College of Oratory," although it was often referred to simply as "the Boston Conservatory" or "the Boston Conservatory of Music."

When Jacchia died in 1932, **Albert Alphin**, a graduate of the Conservatory, took over the school's day-to-day operations, which he ran from his own business, the National Associated Studios of Music, Inc. Alphin later struck a deal with Agide's widow, **Ester Ferrabini Jacchia**, to legally transfer the school to him.

After taking over the Conservatory from the Jacchia family, Alphin and his board voted on December 13, 1935 to reincorporate and change the name of the school back to its original title, **Boston Conservatory of Music**. It would remain so for several decades without any adjustment, but in the early 1950s and into the 1960s, Alphin added an informal flourish to the name, with official letterhead and publications showing the name as **Boston Conservatory of Music, a College of Music, Drama and Dance**. (The Conservatory became a not-for-profit school in 1936, when Alphin dissolved his business corporations in filings with the Commonwealth of Massachusetts.)

In 1982, under the direction of President **William A. Seymour**, the school's name was officially changed to **The Boston Conservatory**, which remained until 2016, when the institution merged with Berklee and legally became **The Boston Conservatory at Berklee**. Following the merger, the Conservatory opted to formally drop the word "The" from the name for branding and stylistic purposes, thereby presenting the school as **Boston Conservatory at Berklee**.

Introduction

Richard Ortner, President of The Boston Conservatory, 1998–2017

That seals it, I thought with a big smile. Plácido Domingo had just concluded his talk at Harvard by greeting "President Roger Brown of Berklee and President Richard Ortner of The Boston Conservatory," with a reference to future collaboration at Berklee's second campus in Valencia, Spain. One of the most revered artists of our age had just put a very public seal of approval on our merger—and an acknowledgement that our very first new program in Valencia will be a summer opera intensive, alongside Domingo's own Advanced Opera Institute. *How interesting,* I thought, *that Maestro Domingo knows The Boston Conservatory through some of our working alumni in the opera world, of course, but also through his own work with Berklee!*

The merger of The Boston Conservatory and Berklee is the latest and surely the most significant "reinvention" of the Conservatory in our time, but transformation is nothing new for us. That capacity—that appetite for reimagining ourselves—has been a hallmark of the Conservatory's personality throughout our 150-year history. For me, the merger would be our way, in our time, of allowing the *idea* of the Conservatory to evolve and flourish.

150 Stories gives us an opportunity to look at that idea as never before.

Some think of the Conservatory as a "place" (and yes, we love our historic buildings on the Fenway, and our new facilities as well), but the school has occupied many places in the city over its long life. It is not just a place, nor is it any one teacher, program, or student. The Boston Conservatory is every teacher, every student; it is all of our programs. It's those who have become Trustees and Overseers and friends of the Conservatory. It's alumni who work actively in music and dance and theater, and equally those who start their own businesses or become teachers, attorneys, photographers, writers, bankers, florists—you name it! It's about people who found their voices here. It's a unique history of innovation, expansion, and exploration of what it means to be a conservatory.

Ask ten people what a conservatory is and you'll get ten different answers. You'll likely get some agreement on the basics: certainly, it's a deep dive into craft—into technique and repertoire, and into the history and language of the art form. It's a place where the great sophisticated stylistic traditions of Western performance art are taught, understood, and absorbed. It's a cloister where, for a few precious years, a gifted few create a unique community— a family of like-minded souls.

It's also a place where teachers are alert to the lived experience and new realities of their exciting young charges, creating experiences for them that mirror their times and allowing them to find themselves as artists. This book shares 150 stories of Boston Conservatory students and teachers who were and are very much alive in their own time—and this Conservatory's history of being right there with them.

Read about Dabney Montgomery—a dance student who became one of the storied Tuskegee Airmen—and how he met Reverend Dr. Martin Luther King, Jr. in Boston and became a powerful civil rights advocate. Read about violist Lorraine Hunt Lieberson, who began singing while a student at the Conservatory and became one of the most celebrated mezzo-sopranos of her generation. Read about jazz legend "Slam" Stewart, who pioneered his signature gift of singing an octave above his dynamic bass playing while at the Conservatory.

In piecing together our history, we see proof of this dynamism in every generation. At our founding in 1867, Julius Eichberg had an idea: he determined that his conservatory would honor the European conventions, but with a distinctly progressive, American accent. He promoted the startling idea that women and African Americans should have access to rigorous, first-rate classical training and professional opportunity, marking him not just a visionary arts leader, but a distinctly *Boston* arts leader.

In the 1920s, the idea expanded again, with the creation of the first Grand Opera department anywhere in the country. And again, in 1943, with the establishment of the first complete dance program that insisted not only on ballet, but on the very new territory of modern dance. And again in the mid-1980s, with the transformation of a drama program into one of the country's first musical theater departments. And yet again in 2011, as the Dance

Division prospered under new leadership, becoming the country's premier program for contemporary dance.

And here we are today. The latest iteration of the idea—our merger with Berklee—says that we are both custodians of great and important traditions and explorers, pioneers in the place where those traditions meet the world we live in, creating the future of these art forms. This current iteration of the idea is not yet one year old, but shows once again that we're actively reinventing our Conservatory, marshaling the resources of today's visionary faculty and students to create something new in the world: Boston Conservatory at Berklee.

We continue today to ask that essential question: What does it mean to be a conservatory? What's being conserved? Is it just the core canon of Western concert music and dance and theater, seen through a contemporary lens, with new technology? Or is it more? Shouldn't it be an idea about the active embrace of all the riches of world storytelling, newly available to us in the digital era? Isn't it about the ability to

create new art forms, using new platforms to communicate what's crucially important to us? For me, *that's* what we conserve: the idea that art is the crucial mirror of human experience and of the times we live in. That, no matter the art form, no matter the century, all art—to paraphrase Richard Rodriguez—is about one thing: what it feels like to be alive. Indeed, our work at the Conservatory celebrates what it feels like to live, to love, to be joyful, to mourn, to die; what it feels like to be young, to be old, to be male or female, to be black or brown or white.

At The Boston Conservatory, throughout our history, we have asked our students to use every bit of their passion and creativity to do just that, and to hold up that mirror for us. So—here's a toast to the imagination and hard work and sheer gumption of those who created (and re-created!) The Boston Conservatory before us, and a rallying cry to the generations to come. Make art for the time you live in, and keep reinventing The Boston Conservatory!

April 2016

The First Hundred Years

1867–1966

Boston Conservatory was born into a world awakening.

In the first half of the nineteenth century, Boston had experienced an era of economic and population growth. Rivers that connected Boston to surrounding regions, an expanding railroad system, and the construction of new roads enabled the city's prolific trade and commerce, securing it as one of largest manufacturing centers in the nation by mid-century.

Beginning in the 1840s, Boston's population began to swell with an influx of immigrants from Ireland, soon followed by Canada, Italy, Eastern Europe, and Russia, and this would continue throughout the remainder of the century. In addition, Boston was known as a center for the abolitionist movement and was headquarters to the Massachusetts branch of the New England Anti-Slavery Society.

Thriving trade and a growing, diverse population helped position Boston for the period of "high culture" that would mark the second half of the nineteenth century. From the mid to late 1800s, much attention and emphasis was placed on literary culture and arts patronage, driven largely by the city's Brahmin movement—an elite, aristocratic-like group that advocated ideals of social cultivation, dignity, and personal virtue. As the Brahmins flourished in Boston, so did education and the arts. The Boston Female Medical School—the nation's first medical school for women, which later merged with Boston University—opened

in 1848; The Boston Public Library, which is the oldest free library in the United States, was founded in 1852; Boston College was founded by Jesuits in 1863; Massachusetts Institute of Technology opened in 1865; Boston Conservatory of Music opened in 1867, followed two weeks later by the New England Conservatory of Music; The Museum of Fine Arts opened in 1876; Emerson College opened in 1880; the Boston Symphony Orchestra was founded in 1881; and Simmons College, an all-female school, opened in 1899.

The American Civil War (1861–1865), which occurred in the midst of this cultural awakening, had significant impact on the city of Boston for years following. It is thought to have improved the city's relations with immigrant populations, who fought and died with Union armies, and it helped raise the status of women, who—in the absence of men who were away serving in battle—filled critical roles and carried out important tasks.

When Boston Conservatory founder Julius Eichberg set out to establish a school of advanced training for gifted violinists just three years after the Civil War ended, Boston was socially and economically ripe, with an appetite for reconstruction, cultural enrichment, and social progress. Eichberg would take advantage of the city's shift, and pursue ideas that even at the time were considered by many to be radical, opening his school's doors to women and recently emancipated African Americans. And such was the first era of the Boston Conservatory—marked by boldness, innovation, and a forward-thinking move towards equality.

Julius Eichberg

Renowned violinist and composer **Julius Eichberg** founded Boston Conservatory of Music on February 11, 1867 at 154 Tremont Street as a professional training academy and community music school. Believed to be the first conservatory established in the United States, the news was heralded as an important moment in both the nation's history and Boston's, as American musicians would for the first time have access to conservatory-style musical training. The Conservatory's opening marked just the beginning of the history Eichberg would make in the last decades of the nineteenth century.

Boston Conservatory of Music was one of the first conservatories to grant admission to African Americans and women. In 1873, Eichberg's operetta, *The Doctor of Alcantara*, was performed by the first African American opera company in the United States. And, in 1878, the maestro established the first-ever professional female quartet—the **Eichberg String Quartet**—so that "all of his students could have a chance to perform professionally," as he noted in a program from an early concert.

Born in Germany, Eichberg first attracted widespread attention at the age of 7 when he performed for **Czar Nicholas I** of Russia at a court concert and, upon the recommendation of **Felix Mendelssohn**, entered the Brussels Conservatoire. By 1859, Eichberg was a leading figure in the Boston music community: he was the *chef d'orchestre*, or "conductor," at the Boston Museum, and in 1867—the same year that he founded Boston Conservatory of Music—he became the supervisor of music for Boston Public Schools, a position he would hold for decades.

When Eichberg died in January 1893, six of Boston's leading newspapers carried the story, and hundreds of students, friends, and Boston residents attended his funeral to mourn his passing. In his eulogy for Eichberg, Reverend Minot J. Savage said of his late friend: "He was an artist; that means that he could not only love and appreciate, but could create the beautiful. He loved his art, and with his devotion he made it respected by his connection to it. He loved all [of] the sister arts, as he counted them as one family. His was the artistic nature on all of its manifold sides."

Eichberg is buried at Mount Auburn Cemetery in Massachusetts.

Yours very truly

Julius Eichberg

Boston Conservatory of Music.

LA
PAVANE
FOR
Violin and Piano
BY
JULIUS EICHBERG.

N.B.
Pavane is the name of a French Court Dance of the XVIII Century

BOSTON
White & Goullaud
86 Tremont St.

The Doctor of Alcantara

In 2008, nearly 135 years after the debut of *The Doctor of Alcantara*, the Music Center at Strathmore in Washington, D.C. staged an evening to celebrate the groundbreaking two-act comic opera. When **Julius Eichberg** wrote *The Doctor of Alcantara* in 1862, he could not have imagined the trajectory his work would have.

The two-act, English-language comic opera featuring a libretto by **Benjamin E. Wolff** was first performed at the Boston Museum on Tremont Street, where Eichberg was the *chef d'orchestre* (conductor). The piece was written to be performed by professional and amateur companies alike, as was customary in the late nineteenth century in the United States.

Eichberg—whose operas also include *A Night in Rome* (1864), *The Rose of Tyrol* (1865), and *The Two Cadis* (1868)—often conducted the piece and continued to tinker with its score through the first year of performances.

From the first performances in the 1860s, *The Doctor of Alcantara* was welcomed by audiences in Boston and Washington D.C., and soon after had an acclaimed run in New York City at the Bowery Theatre for sixteen performances. The 1873 production, too, would head to New York City for eight performances before returning to Washington for an "encore" run that May.

What forever burnished the opera in history, however, came in 1873, when Eichberg selected the piece to be the first fully staged opera performed by African American singers, led by musical director **John Esputa**. An advertisement in the January 28, 1873 edition of *The Washington Evening Times* boasted that the Original Colored American Opera Company "numbering over forty voices and made up of the very best musical talent, is the only opera combination composed exclusively of colored ladies and gentlemen ever organized in this or any other country."

The first performances in Lincoln Hall, held on Monday, February 2 and Tuesday, February 3, 1873, were standing room only. Washington-area newspapers sent their opera critics to write about the performances both as a cultural phenomenon and a musical event.

The Washington Evening Star's unsigned piece on February 4 read: "The announcement of the intended performance of The Doctor of Alcantara by a colored opera company at Lincoln Hall last evening attracted a very large audience, embracing nearly all the leading colored people of the District and many of our prominent white citizens ... For a first performance it was a decided success, and the choruses were given with a force and precision which has not been excelled by any company which has sung the opera in this city ... It would not be fair with the disadvantages of a first appearance and the limited stage accommodations at Lincoln Hall, to judge these performers by the highest professional standard, but ... [it] gives promise of better things in the future." The world took notice. *The New York Times* wrote on its front page of February 5, 1873, "The opera *The Doctor of Alcantara* was performed last night in Washington, by a company of colored singers, composed of singers in St. Martin's Catholic Church, of that city."

The opera was first published in 1879 by O. Ditson & Co., located next door to the Conservatory's original location on Tremont Street, and republished in 1904 as *The Doctor of Alcantara, A Comic Opera in Two Acts*.

For more than two decades after Eichberg's death, his family allowed the use of the work as a fundraising tool for Boston youth programs. In 1916, *The Boston Globe* announced, "The Lend-a-Hand Dramatic Club of Greater Boston presented Julius Eichberg's opera, *The Doctor of Alcantara*, in Jordan Hall ... The proceeds will be devoted to the vacation camp for girls, which the club has at Ashland."

NEW ENLARGED AND REVISED EDITION.

THE DOCTOR OF
ALCANTARA
COMIC OPERA.

LIBRETTO BY

MUSIC BY

BENJ. E. WOOLF.

JULIUS EICHBERG.

ACT 1ST.

CHORUSES, 50cts.

COMPLETE, $1.50

BOSTON

OLIVER DITSON & CO.,

The Quartets

From the first days of Boston Conservatory of Music, forward-thinking founder **Julius Eichberg** created a supportive environment for his students, seeking out paid performance opportunities for them and ensuring that they were studying under the best instructors. That was true in 1879 when he founded the **Eichberg Quartet**, also known as the Eichberg Ladies' String Quartet or the Eichberg Quartette.

The original Eichberg Quartet, believed to be the first-ever, all-female professional string quartet, was comprised of Conservatory students **Lillian Shattuck** (violin), **Lillian Chandler** (violin), **Abbie Shepardson** (viola), and **Lettie Launder** (cello). Over the years, iterations of the quartet included **Idalian Howard** (violin), **Emma Grebe** (viola), **Jennie Daniell** (viola), **Laura Webster** (cello), and **Alice Gray Lathrop** (cello).

In 1881, Eichberg sent the quartet to Berlin for a year of study, where they performed and received positive reviews from the critics of the day. The boldness of the creation of the quartet was not lost on Eichberg, who wrote in an 1879 article titled "Lady Violinists" that "we should be remiss in failing to credit our female students with at least an equal degree of talent, industry, and success. We gladly espouse the cause of women's right to play upon all the instruments of the orchestra."

In her book, *Unsung: A History of Women in American Music*, **Christine Ammer** writes that Eichberg actively created opportunities for women, even when others were refusing to train them as professional musicians. **Olive Mead**, who began studying with Eichberg at the age of 7 before studying under **Franz Kneisel**, was one of many to benefit from Eichberg's progressive thinking. In 1903, she founded the Olive Mead Quartet, whose other members included **Vera Fonaroff**, **Gladys North**, and **Lillian Littlehales**. Eichberg also taught cellist **Georgia Pray Lasselle**, who would later join the American String Quartette. His other protégée, violinist and conductor **Caroline B. Nichols**, went on to form The Fadettes of Boston, a highly successful all-women orchestra that performed for thirty years.

Eichberg's tradition continues today with **The Julius Quartet**, which was formed at the Conservatory in 2012 by **Hyun Jeong "Helen" Lee** (B.M. '15, violin), **David Do** (B.M. '14, violin), **John Batchelder** (B.M. '12, G.P.D. '14, viola), and **Byron Hogan** (G.P.D. '14, cello). In 2016, The Julius Quartet was in residence at the John J. Cali School of Music at Montclair State University, where they worked with the Shanghai Quartet. While at the Conservatory, the Julius Quartet served as the school's prestigious Honors String Quartet. The group performed numerous concerts to critical acclaim and were nominated for the Harvard Musical Association's Arthur Foote Award by the Conservatory's then-Music Division Director **Abra K. Bush**. According to the Julius Quartet, "Our name honors what [Eichberg] believed in for the arts, as well as being an ode to where we were first formed."

Lower left: Eichberg Quartette program cover, circa 1882; *Lower right*: The Julius Quartet: John Batchelder, Hyun Jeong "Helen" Lee, Byron Hogan, and David Do

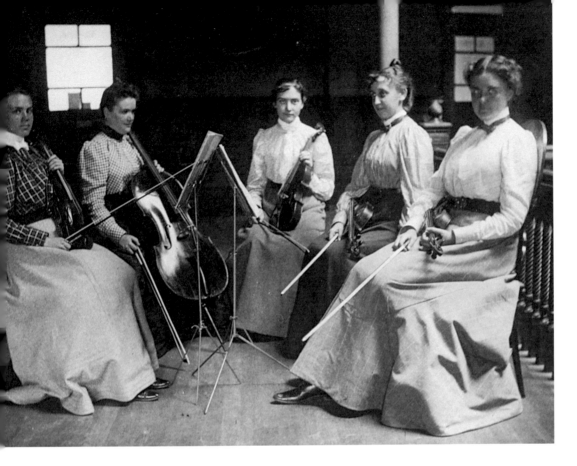

Eichberg String Quartette.

Lillian Shattuck · Violin.
Lettie Launder · Violin.
Emma Grebe · Viola.
Laura Webster · Cello.

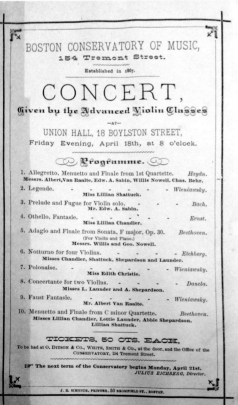

BOSTON CONSERVATORY OF MUSIC,
154 Tremont Street.

Established in 1867.

CONCERT,

Given by the Advanced Violin Classes

—AT—

UNION HALL, 18 BOYLSTON STREET,

Friday Evening, April 18th, at 8 o'clock.

Programme.

1. Allegretto, Menuetto and Finale from 1st Quartette. *Haydn.*
Messrs. Albert, Van Raalte, Edw. A. Sabin, Willis Nowell, Chas. Behr.

2. Legende. — *Wieniawsky.*
Miss Lillian Shattuck.

3. Prelude and Fugue for Violin solo. — *Bach.*
Mr. Edw. A. Sabin.

4. Othello, Fantasie. — *Ernst.*
Miss Lillian Chandler.

5. Adagio and Finale from Sonata, F major, Op. 30. *Beethoven.*
(For Violin and Piano.)
Messrs. Willis and Geo. Nowell.

6. Notturno for four Violins. — *Eichberg.*
Misses Chandler, Shattuck, Shepardson and Launder.

7. Polonaise. — *Wieniawsky.*
Miss Edith Christie.

8. Concertante for two Violins. — *Dancla.*
Misses L. Launder and A. Shepardson.

9. Faust Fantasie. — *Wieniawsky.*
Mr. Albert Van Raalte.

10. Menuetto and Finale from C minor Quartette. *Beethoven.*
Misses Lillian Chandler, Lettie Launder, Abbie Shepardson,
Lillian Shattuck.

TICKETS, 50 CTS. EACH.

To be had at O. DITSON & CO., WHITE, SMITH & CO., at the door, and the Office of the
CONSERVATORY, 154 Tremont Street.

☞ The next term of the Conservatory begins Monday, April 21st.
JULIUS EICHBERG, Director.

J. E. SIMONDS, PRINTER, 50 BROMFIELD ST., BOSTON.

Lillian Shattuck

Lillian Shattuck's storied career was the result of talent, years of training, and hard work, but this masterful violinist credited her success to the support of her teacher, Conservatory founder **Julius Eichberg**.

Eichberg selected the 15-year-old Canton, Massachusetts native for Boston Conservatory of Music and gave her a solo in the school's second public concert, for which *The Boston Globe* praised her precision. He again featured Shattuck in 1879, when he created the first all-female professional string quartet. The other

Conservatory students in the **Eichberg Quartet**—also known as the Eichberg Ladies' String Quartet and the Eichberg Quartette—were **Lillian Chandler** (violin), **Abbie Shepardson** (viola), and **Lettie Launder** (cello).

Shattuck continued to perform as a member of the quartet for years after Eichberg's death in 1893, later becoming a noted pedagogue in Boston. She taught countless violinists from her studio in the Pierce Building in Copley Square until her death in 1940.

Henry C. Brown

Though the newspapers lauded **Henry C. Brown** as a successful real estate speculator at the time of his death in December 1912 at the age of 74, Brown had also enjoyed a vibrant career as one of the country's most celebrated cornetists and sought-after teachers.

Brown's professional career began when he was 15 years old, playing cornet as part of the orchestra for the National Theatre on Portland Street in Boston's old West End. In the mid-1850s, Brown became a deputy leader of the Boston Brigade Band, and during the Civil War he organized a band attached to the 23rd Regiment Massachusetts Volunteer Infantry.

It was at the Battle of New Bern, North Carolina, in 1862 that Brown "was pressed into military duty, along with all the other players," according to a news account of the time.

In November 1875, when the remains of Natick-born **Henry Wilson**, the vice president of the United States, were brought up from Washington, D.C., Brown played Schubert's *Elegy of Tears* as the funeral procession entered the Massachusetts State House.

Brown was hired by **Julius Eichberg** for a stretch at the Boston Conservatory of Music, where his students would include famed bandleader **Perry George "P. G." Lowery**, the first African American to complete his training at the Conservatory. Brown's other students at this time included **Ezra Bagley**, the first principal trumpet of the Boston Symphony Orchestra from 1881 to 1886, and **Florence Louise Horne**, who among her many accomplishments, toured with the all-women orchestra, The Fadettes of Boston.

As Brown's playing and teaching career was winding down, he "made profitable real estate investments," according to his obituary in *The Boston Globe*. Those holdings included his home at 41 Mount Vernon Street in Beacon Hill.

Top: Henry C. Brown's Boston cornet, circa 1866; *Bottom:* Led by Henry C. Brown, the Boston Brigade Band performs at Quincy Market in celebration of the market's fiftieth anniversary in 1876.

Perry George "P. G." Lowery

Perry George "P. G." Lowery boarded a train in his native Kansas and arrived at Boston Conservatory of Music on May 22, 1887 with little fanfare but high expectations.

The cornet prodigy, then just 18 years old, came to Boston at the invitation of the Conservatory's founder, **Julius Eichberg**, to study on a full scholarship with famed cornetist **Henry C. Brown**, who called Lowery "the world's greatest colored cornet soloist," according to biographer **Clifford E. Watkins**, who wrote *Showman: The Life and Music of Perry George Lowery*. (In 1902, Lowery wrote home that Brown had given him a special Boston Cornet, proclaiming it the best instrument he had ever played.)

Lowery lived up to the hopes of Eichberg, Brown, and many others through a career that took him around the country, to Europe, and often back to Eureka, Kansas. In his time, Lowery earned a reputation as a bandleader and for running the "sideshow" orchestras and bands for some of the biggest circuses in the country.

When Lowery received his diploma from the Conservatory after "completing a full course of study," he was the first African American graduate of the school, as he would later describe it to a newspaper interviewer. Lowery's half-brother, the noted trombonist **Ed Greene**, traveled with him and also took classes at the Conservatory.

Among his many friends and fellow musicians, one stood out: **Scott Joplin**, the acclaimed pianist who was dubbed the "King of Ragtime" and recorded Lowery's version of Joplin's "The Sunflower Slow Drag" in 1921.

According to Kansas census records, Lowery was born in Kansas in 1869 to a family of farmers who were also known as talented musicians. Prior to his Boston move, Lowery played in local shows but had reportedly never taken a formal lesson.

After his Conservatory studies, Lowery put his training and considerable talent to immediate use. In 1894, he played for thirty-two weeks in Kansas City with a

P.G. Lowery with the Barnum & Bailey Circus sideshow band

theater troupe and began touring a short time later. Over the course of his lengthy career, Lowery was a soloist, composer, conductor, manager, and bandleader.

By the end of World War I, Lowery had made a name for himself as a musician, but had tired of being on the road. A solution was provided by fellow Kansan **Merle Evans**, director of the Ringling Brothers and Barnum & Bailey Circus Band, who "recruited Lowery to direct the sideshow band," according to the Kansas Historical Society.

Lowery led the Ringling Brothers sideshow band from 1920 to 1923, and again from 1926 to 1931, according to the circus

company's archive. Evans pushed circus management to transfer Lowery to the big-top band, but the company was unwilling to challenge the dictates of segregation, records show. In a twist, the circus management paid Lowery the salary he would have received in the main tent, something he shared with his band's musicians, who called him "Professor Lowery" for his education and strict adherence to conservatory standards.

"Among African-American bandmasters, few could rival the talent and influence of Perry George Lowery," wrote **Lynn Abbott** and **Doug Seroff** in their book, *Ragged But Right*. "Over his long career in minstrel shows, circuses, and vaudeville, Lowery

trained and employed hundreds of musicians and helped create opportunities for countless black entertainers."

During the height of his career it seemed as though Lowery's every move was chronicled in the newspapers, but his death, ironically, went largely unnoticed. He died in 1942 in Cleveland, Ohio, and his family buried him in an unmarked grave.

Boston Conservatory Leaders

Julius Eichberg

R. Marriner Floyd

Herman P. Chelius

As the director of the Boston Museum Orchestra and the supervisor of music in the City of Boston's public high schools, **Julius Eichberg** was already a leader in Boston's thriving classical music community and at the vanguard of music education when he founded Boston Conservatory of Music in 1867. Officially listed on all documents (and the newspaper ads for the school) as the president, Eichberg was so much more: he served as music director, conductor, and host for all Conservatory concerts, as well as the resident composer and arranger. His younger brother, **Isidor Eichberg**, aided him in the day-to-day management of the Conservatory. Isidor was the school's secretary and, by all accounts, took care of everything that was not related to music.

Following Julius's unexpected death in 1893, Isidor ran the school for about a year, until his own death, whereupon Julius's wife, **Sophie**, and daughter, then **Annie Eichberg King**, transferred the ownership of the Conservatory to **R. Marriner Floyd**, a watchmaker and jewelry store proprietor who also advertised himself as a "purveyor of fine

musical instruments." It was a convenient arrangement, as Floyd's shop was just down the hall from the Conservatory's fourth floor classrooms at 154 Tremont Street.

Floyd immediately enlisted a noted Boston organist and choir director, **Herman P. Chelius**, who had been hired by Eichberg as an instructor in 1880, to oversee music instruction. During this time, the school expanded its class offerings and gained a reputation for piano training and vocal instruction, with a focus on choral and ensemble music training.

The reorganization of Boston Conservatory of Music under Floyd was announced in *The Boston Sunday Post* on June 21, 1896, under the headline, "Boston Conservatory Now a Corporation." The story begins: "Perhaps the most important musical event of the week was the incorporation of the Boston Conservatory of Music under the laws of Massachusetts."

The documents from that first reorganization also listed "Professor Floyd" as president; Chelius as musical director; **Dr. Percy Goetschius**, a well-known Boston

teacher affiliated with the New England Conservatory, as Boston Conservatory's vice president; and **Susan E. Stevens** as treasurer. The newspaper story said that boards of directors and trustees would be named later, but no records could be found of such a board existing at that time.

The Conservatory finalized its new corporation through a filing with the Commonwealth in 1905. On August 15, 1914, Floyd further muddled the school's name when he filed to reestablish it as The Boston Conservatory of Music and College of Oratory. However, the name appears to have been largely ignored by the school's students, the Boston community, and newspapers, who continued to use "Boston Conservatory of Music" when referring to the institution.

Floyd's many changes to the school contributed to a period of uncertainty for the Conservatory community, as evidenced in a program booklet note written years later for the grand opening of 31 Hemenway Street: "[Floyd's reign] included several unsettled years, during which reorganization was affected in 1905,

Agide Jacchia

Ester Ferrabini Jacchia

Albert Alphin

1914, and 1920." The latter date was a turning point for the Conservatory, as it marked Floyd's passing and the board's appointment of Boston Pops Orchestra conductor **Agide Jacchia** as the new director. His wife, famed opera singer **Ester Ferrabini Jacchia**, also joined the faculty. "Mr. Jacchia's knowledge and wide experience proved of inestimable value in reestablishing the prestige of the school," according to the program notes from the opening event for 31 Hemenway.

The Italian-born Jacchia had come to live in Boston only two years prior, when he was named conductor of the Boston Pops Orchestra in 1917. In 1920, he turned his attention to reviving the Conservatory. Like his musical predecessors, Jacchia shifted the school's focus to his area of expertise: opera. The magazine *Musical America* wrote of Jacchia's vision: "The school will offer instruction in all the usual branches of music, but the director considers that its most striking feature will be the complete course of training for grand opera."

In addition to his wife, Jacchia added a number of notable musicians, arrangers, and singers to his faculty roster. He continued to run the school and live in Boston until poor health prompted him to return to Italy in 1928 and, later, to a series of resorts, seeking a cure. Although he only returned to Boston for a few months at a time, Jacchia was able to keep the school running efficiently "by mail and telegraph up to nearly the very end," according to a 1966 Conservatory history.

Following his death in Italy in 1932, Jacchia's widow, Ester, returned to Boston for a short time to run the school and continue teaching. She ultimately returned to Italy and the school was run by **Albert Alphin**, an alumnus and former faculty member, until he took ownership of the Conservatory a couple of years later. In 1936, Alphin moved to dissolve the Conservatory as a business corporation and reestablished it as a nonprofit educational organization.

No one except Eichberg had a greater impact in the first one hundred years of the Conservatory than Alphin did. Already a student at the Conservatory when Jacchia took over, Alphin studied piano, organ, theory, and composition, according to Conservatory records. In 1924, Alphin was appointed to the faculty and continued to teach through 1927, when he founded the National Associated Studios of Music, a few doors from the Conservatory down Huntington Avenue, just across from Symphony Hall.

Alphin's commitment to the Conservatory never waned. Over the years, he organized numerous alumni events and concerts in Boston. For the school's 125th anniversary celebration, **H. Wilfred Churchill**, an alumnus who joined the faculty upon his graduation in 1934, wrote of Alphin's early days running the school: "Mr. Alphin, of course, was the only administrator … he was the secretary, treasurer, registrar, and sometimes he was the janitor!" By the late 1940s, Alphin had expanded the management of the school to include **Albert C. Sherman**, dean of students; **Elaine Fairfield**, registrar; and **Lois Tido**, secretary.

Alphin also added faculty and actively looked to expand the Conservatory's offerings. It was Alphin who convinced

H. Wilfred Churchill

George A. Brambilla

William A. Seymour

famed dancer **Jan Veen** to move his dance school to become part of the Conservatory and brought on **Harlan F. Grant** to run the drama program, as it was then called. It was also Alphin who moved the campus to the Fenway. After World War II, he was finally able to get the construction of 31 Hemenway underway, and when the building opened in 1949, it was celebrated by the whole community. The Board of Trustees, which hosted the opening concert and ceremony, was led by its president **Reverend Arthur B. Whitney**, members **Leslie Babbin**, **Elaine Fairfield**, **Thomas F. True**, drama department head Grant, and ex-officio Alphin.

When the Conservatory marked its centennial in 1967, Alphin announced his retirement and appointed **George A. Brambilla** as the school's director. Alphin would continue to serve as the school's secretary and maintained a presence at the Conservatory until his death in 1973.

Brambilla, who held a bachelor of music and master of music in music composition from Boston University, had served as dean of the Conservatory under Alphin. Prior to joining the Conservatory, Brambilla was dean of Berklee School of Music from

1960 to 1963. He worked for many years as a pianist, arranger, and composer in the radio, television, and recording industries before entering academia. Brambilla is credited with expanding the Conservatory's curriculum offerings and refocusing some of its programs. Perhaps most notable was his establishment of the Conservatory's opera training program in 1973, led by **John Moriarty**. After retiring in 1979, Brambilla became a partner at the Falcone Piano Manufacturing Company in Haverhill, Massachusetts, and died in 2010 at the age of 82.

Brambilla hired **Herbert J. Philpott** as the Conservatory's dean. Philpott was a trombone player and a noted member of Boston's music education community. He earned a bachelor of arts and master of arts in music from Boston University. Philpott served as dean of the Conservatory from 1967 to 1977. He was 81 years old when he died in December 2014.

In 1979, **Dale A. DuVall** was appointed by the board to run the Conservatory in what would become a period of great instability for the school. DuVall, who had a master of business administration from Northeastern University but no music or arts training, was

derisively referred to as "the accountant." In March of 1980, the Conservatory faced legal action from the City of Boston for 132 building code violations in 5 dormitories along the Fenway strip: 24, 26, 32, 40, and 54. The Conservatory's Student Council, led by its president **Steven Rosen**, a musical theater student from Los Angeles, protested the conditions. To fix the dormitories, they enlisted the school's then 1,600-member Alumni Association, for which **Armand Dilan** (M.M. '76) served as president and **Carmen Perrone** (B.M. '77) as executive director. That alliance would come into play again just a year later, when the Conservatory faced losing its accreditation.

It was at this time that former associate dean **William A. Seymour** agreed to return to the school at the request of the Board of Trustees to oversee the changes required to allow the Conservatory to keep its accreditation. (Seymour had joined the Conservatory in 1967, teaching music education and directing the chorale, and later serving as associate dean.) Seymour's connection to the school, along with the support of faculty, students, and alumni, allowed him to steer the school back from the brink of closure.

Richard Ortner

David Scott Sloan

Mimi Hewlett

When DuVall was asked to resign in 1981, the board again turned to Seymour—this time naming him president of the Conservatory. "Seymour accepted the presidency of the Boston Conservatory in a moment of great crisis for the institution, which could have folded," reporter **Richard Dyer** wrote in a 1998 *Boston Globe* article. "Seymour's leadership of [the] board, faculty, and student body enabled the school to survive the crisis and emerge on new footing." Among the many advancements credited to Seymour was the upgrade and redesign of the school's course catalogs, and the expansion of student recruitment to include the entire United States, as well as Asia.

Seymour announced his retirement in 1997 and stepped down at the close of the academic year, but continued his affiliation with the Conservatory. "I have agreed to help my successor for a year and see our regular accreditation process through," Seymour told the *Globe*. Among those to serve as chairs of the Board of Trustees during Seymour's tenure were: **Franklin Warren Hobbs**, who served as a trustee for eighteen years; and **Robert Montcrieff**, who also served as a trustee for eighteen years.

Following Seymour's retirement, the Conservatory's Board of Trustees, led by cochairs **JoAnne W. Dickinson**, **Gary R. Mikula**, and **Anthony Pangaro**, named **Richard Ortner** as the Conservatory's president. Ortner came to the Conservatory in July 1998 after a remarkable twenty-three-year career with the Boston Symphony Orchestra, which included serving as administrator of the Tanglewood Music Center, the Symphony's summer institute for advanced musical training in the Berkshires.

Ortner's tenure at the Conservatory was marked by a number of innovations, expansions, and redefining programs that included reconfiguring of the Dance Division to focus on contemporary dance, expanding the music education program to offer training for instructing autistic students, and overseeing further development of the musical theater program to international acclaim.

Ortner also enacted a plan to improve the physical campus. The initiative included a renovation of the now more than fifty-year-old 31 Hemenway Street building, as well as construction of the 132 Ipswich Street facility, which won raves from architecture

critics and, more importantly, the students and staff who use it. "It really is a remarkable thing to see the Conservatory create from 2014 to 2016 something in this way," said **David Scott Sloan**, chairman of the Board of Trustees, who credits Ortner and former board chairman, **Alfred D. Houston**, with getting the project completed.

Shortly after Ortner became president, **James L. Burns** was elected as chairman of the trustees and served in that capacity for a year and a half. Burns was followed by **Mimi Hewlett**, who held more than fifteen years of service on the board, including six as chair. Houston served as chairman for six years and Sloan was board chair for three.

In 2016, Ortner and his Berklee counterpart, **Roger H. Brown**, announced a merger that would bring the two schools, longtime neighbors in the city's Fenway neighborhood, together, resulting in Boston Conservatory at Berklee.

R. (Roscoe) Marriner Floyd

Patent for Amplification Device, 1916

R. (Roscoe) Marriner Floyd, second president of Boston Conservatory of Music, assumed the presidency, while owning a business in the same building as the Conservatory. Floyd, who had an interest in musical instruments and invention, created multiple designs and patents for sound amplification. The 1916 patent shown here details an invention engineered to amplify sound produced by the body of a wooden instrument, such as a violin. It is unclear whether his invention was ever developed and manufactured, but based on audio and recording records of the time, it was in line with other types of sound engineering innovations being created at the time.

R. M. FLOYD.

METHOD OF AND MEANS FOR INCREASING THE RESONANCE OF SOUND MODIFYING WOODEN BODIES.

APPLICATION FILED JUNE 8, 1915.

1,197,116.

Patented Sept. 5, 1916.

2 SHEETS—SHEET 2.

Fig. 2.

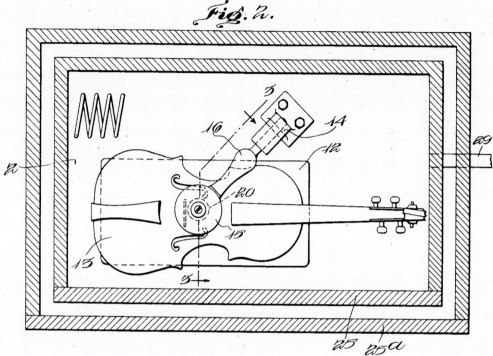

Fig. 5.

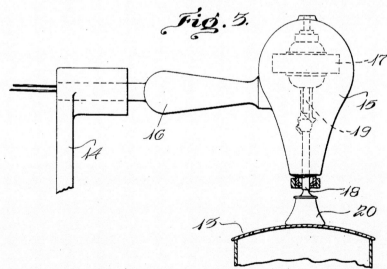

Witnesses:

Ernest A. Telfer

Forrest R. Ronlstone

Inventor

R. M. Floyd

by Wright Brown Quinby May

Attys.

Class of 1897

The class of 1897 stands out in the Conservatory's history. The forty-eight musicians and singers who made up the class included the names of some of the city's leading families at the time, including Spaulding, Morse, Logan, and Gilbert. The graduation exercises were covered by the local press, reinforcing the Conservatory's place in Boston education and the arts. The Conservatory's class that year was predominantly women, which stood in stark contrast to other schools in Boston at the end of the nineteenth century.

The Boston Daily Globe of June 21, 1897 reported that the Conservatory's associate director **George H. Howard** "made some interesting remarks" and school president, **R. Marriner Floyd**, wished "godspeed to the class, which is one of the largest the [C]onservatory has ever sent forth" at the Chickering Hall, Huntington Avenue proceedings, "which was crowded by the friends of the fair graduates."

The Smoking Lawsuit

Boston Conservatory v. Ary Dulfer

During his time leading the Conservatory, **Agide Jacchia** was known for his high standards for faculty classroom conduct, and his stance forced him to face, and ultimately lose, a lawsuit. The case was Boston Conservatory of Music v. **Ary Dulfer**, one of the earliest cases in which smoking cigarettes in the workplace was the subject of a legal debate.

When Dulfer, a well-known Boston concert violinist and Conservatory teacher, first sued Jacchia and the Conservatory in the mid-1920s, it was filed as a simple case of employee conduct and a dispute over the collection of teaching fees. History, however, remembers the 1926 Supreme Judicial Court ruling by Massachusetts' highest court for its early legal references of smoking being banned in the workplace, several decades before the Massachusetts legislature formally voted to ban smoking in the workplace.

More than two years before the case would wind its way through the court system, Jacchia had written a letter to Dulfer reprimanding him for ignoring the Conservatory's smoking regulations. It read, in part: "It is just one week since I wrote you calling your attention to the well-known regulation of the [C]onservatory prohibiting smoking in the lesson rooms, and admonishing you that I insisted upon its strict observance." Soon after, Dulfer was discharged as a teacher "because he insisted on smoking at the Conservatory while giving lessons," according to a June 4, 1926 report on the court case in *The Boston Globe*.

After his official discharge in 1924, Dulfer continued to teach about ten or so students at his studio on Hemenway Street, just around the corner from the Conservatory. Jacchia sought to recoup fees that Dulfer collected from Conservatory students, but

Dulfer maintained that he had met the requirements of his contract and did not have to relinquish the fees.

A Suffolk Superior Court jury ruled against Jacchia and the school on issues related to Dulfer's contract and workplace policies, allowing him to keep the fees. The Massachusetts Supreme Judicial Court affirmed the verdict in a ruling issued on May 26, 1926.

The case is remembered today as one of the first that addressed smoking in the workplace.

Top left: Agide Jacchia, 1920; *Lower right:* Ary Dulfer

VIOLINIST WINS IN THE SUPREME COURT

Finding of Jury Upheld Case of Ary Dulfer

The Supreme Court, in a decision handed down today, upholds the finding of a jury in the Superior Court which found for Ary Dulfer, a Boston violinist, who lives at 270 Huntington av, in the suit brought against him by the Boston Conservatory of Music, Inc, to recover several hundred dollars he received from pupils whom he formerly taught at the conservatory.

Mr Dulfer was discharged as a teacher at the Boston Conservatroy of Music by Agide Jacchia, because he insisted on smoking at the conservatory while giving lessons. Dulfer had been originally engaged by Mr Jacchia and his recompense was to be one-half the tuition the conservatory received from pupils he taught.

On Oct 6, 1923, Mr Jacchia wrote to the violin teacher, warning him against smoking during lessons, and on Oct 13 Mr Jacchia wrote again, calling his attention to the previous warning, and stating that as it seemed impossible to obtain his obedience to this regulation, he was asking him to sever his connection with the conservatory on Jan 13, 1924.

After leaving the conservatory Mr Dulfer continued to teach about 10 conservatory pupils, who came to him at his studio, and under a clause with the conservatory "he would pay half of the tuition he received from any conservatory pupils who came to him to the conservatory."

Dulfer claimed that he did not "disconnect himself," and the jury and the Supreme Court upheld him.

Boston Conservatory of Music, Inc.,
Agide Jacchia, Director.
250 Huntington Avenue, Boston 17 Mass.
October 13, 1923.

Mr. Ary Dulfer, 20 Hemenway Street, Boston, Mass.

     Dear Mr. Dulfer: It is just one week since I wrote you, calling your attention to the well-known regulation of the conservatory prohibiting smoking in the lesson rooms, and admonishing you that I insisted upon its strict observance.

     In spite of this warning I have since seen you smoking during lessons and I am therefore convinced of the impossibility of obtaining your obedience to this regulation. According to your contract, therefore, you will kindly consider your connection with the Boston Conservatory of Music termainated three months from date, January 13, 1924.

         Yours sincerely,
         Agide Jacchia.

Formation of the Grand Opera Department

In 1920, **Agide Jacchia** took the helm of the Conservatory after a tumultuous period of leadership under **R. Marriner Floyd**. Jacchia, who came to the United States from Italy in 1918 to conduct for the Boston Pops Orchestra, sought to stabilize the school and shift its focus to his passion: opera. Jacchia's wife, **Ester Ferrabini Jacchia**, was an established opera singer who helped her husband organize the Conservatory's "Grand Opera Department," believed to be the first of its kind in the United States. Today, the Voice / Opera Department remains a staple of the Conservatory's offerings, with a host of successful alumni who have gone on to sing for the Metropolitan Opera, perform with highly respected companies, and assume prestigious pedagogical appointments.

The Boston Conservatory's production of *Transformations* by Conrad Susa, 2012

One Hundred Years of Opera Training

When mezzo-soprano **Sandra Piques Eddy** took the stage in March 2016 in the Boston Lyric Opera's production of Jules Massenet's *Werther*, audiences at the Emerson Colonial Theatre were mesmerized. The success of Eddy (B.M. '94, music education/voice) is a shining example of Boston Conservatory's legacy in the opera world, one that has been secured by a legion of talented alumni and faculty.

The Conservatory's voice and opera program, renowned for its dynamic training and leading faculty, dates to the first days of the school. In Boston Conservatory of Music's advertisements and catalogs in 1867 are listings for voice faculty that include **Auguste Kreissman** and Conservatory founder **Julius Eichberg**. The 1870–1871 academic year brought an expansion of the program with the hiring of **A. Ardavani**, **Bertha Johannsen**, **Carl Pfluegger**, **Hiram Wilde**, and **Solon Wilder**. In 1873, **Nelson Varley**,

a successful Boston conductor, taught voice, and in the 1880s, **Charles F. Webber** and **Villa Whitney White** were listed as instructors.

The arrival of **Agide Jacchia** as the Conservatory's director in 1920 marks a sizeable increase in the prominence of the school's opera training program, largely because Jacchia's directorship meant the Conservatory gained one of the most sought-after opera singers and teachers of the day: Jacchia's wife, **Ester Ferrabini Jacchia**. "The Conservatory was one of the first schools in the country to establish a Grand Opera Department," wrote **Andrea Olmstead**, former chair of music history, in a 1985 historical record of the Conservatory.

One of Ferrabini's first students was **Iride Pilla**, the soprano who later enjoyed a seven-decade career as a teacher at the Conservatory. In 2004, on what would have

been have been Pilla's one hundredth birthday, former students and her many fans gathered to give a concert organized by her studio pianist **Bradley Pennington** (B.M. '86, voice), founder of Boston Bel Canto Opera.

In 1973, the Conservatory's then-director **George Brambilla** refocused some degree programs, which included formalizing the Opera Training Program, led at the time by **John Moriarty**. For a period, Moriarty ran a combined opera program that included students from Boston Conservatory and New England Conservatory. The program took advantage of the best that both schools had to offer, from faculty to facilities, to school-based orchestras. Moriarty was head of this joint program and served as vocal coach and conductor for performances.

The voice/opera faculty has been among the longest serving and closest-knit group

Iride Pilla

Robert Honeysucker

Sandra Piques Eddy

at the Conservatory. Over the years, the faculty has included **Wesley Copplestone**, who taught voice and oratorio from 1944 to 1981; voice teacher and vocal therapist **David Blair McClosky** and his wife, **Barbara McClosky**; **Grace Hunter**, voice, 1946–1987; and **Philine Falco**, voice, 1957–1977.

Many attribute the familial closeness of the Conservatory's opera/voice program to the loyalty of alumni, many of whom returned as guest artists or teachers. One of these includes Pilla's charge **Mary Saunders** (B.M. '74, M.M. '75, voice), who has been on the voice faculty since 1976 and is the former chair of the Voice Department. Another accomplished opera alumna who later taught voice was **Elisabeth Phinney** (Honorary Doctorate '05), who retired in 2005 after thirty-two years at the Conservatory. Known to her students as "Frau" (a nod to her German birth), Phinney's retirement concert was organized

by **Patty Thom**, who assumed the role of chair in 2003 and continues to serve in this capacity as of 2017. The performance featured mezzo-soprano **Sondra Kelly** (B.M. '82, voice), baritone **Robert Honeysucker**, who has been on the voice faculty since 1981, and tenor **John Bernard** (B.M. '96, opera). **Monique Phinney**, Elisabeth's daughter, has also taught private lessons at the Conservatory to classical/opera and musical theater students since 1994, carrying on the family tradition.

Other notable artists trained at the Conservatory include: **Wendy Harmer** (B.M. '03, voice), who has performed with the Metropolitan Opera; and **Lorraine Hunt Lieberson** (M.M. '85, voice) and **Victoria Livengood** (M.M. '85, voice), both of whom were recruited into the program by Moriarty.

Livengood is a 1984 first-place winner of the Metropolitan Opera National Council

Auditions and has performed several leading roles at the Metropolitan Opera, including a role as title character in the 2002 production of George Bizet's *Carmen*, conducted by **Plácido Domingo**. A student of Frau Phinney, Livengood has been twice nominated for Grammy Awards and, in 2017, was featured on a recording that won two Grammys.

More recent graduates of the Conservatory's opera program who have made a splash in the opera world include **Vanessa Becerra** (M.M. '14, opera); **Anna Bridgman** (M.M. '16, opera); **Abigail Dock** (M.M. '15, P.S.C. '17, opera); **Eric Ferring** (M.M. '16, opera); **Anne Maguire** (B.M. '12, voice); **Courtney Miller** (M.M. '11, P.S.C. '12, opera); **Stephen Mumbert** (M.M. '07, voice); **Sherri Seiden** (B.M. '84, voice), who took first place at the 1989 Metropolitan Opera National Council Audition; **Emma Sorenson** (M.M. '15, opera); and **Wei Zheng** (M.M. '09, voice).

Iride Pilla

She was known simply—and almost always—as Miss Pilla. When **Iride Pilla** graduated in 1924, she was hailed as the first "major voice" to graduate from Boston Conservatory. She would go on to establish a successful career as a performer and an influential instructor of voice at the Conservatory for seven decades.

"Singing was not just a question of musicianship, but of character," Pilla told *The Boston Globe*. It was both a performance philosophy and an instructional strategy, and she guided her students as much in the principles of vocal technique as she did in how to behave as a performer, colleague, and citizen. Of diminutive stature but powerful presence, Pilla set high standards for her students in all aspects of their public lives. A multitude

of former students proudly claim their time with the exacting teacher. They include **Christine Whittlesey**, **Roberta Laws**, **Catherine Lamy**, **Lizbeth Brittain**, former Boston Conservatory Voice Department Chair **Mary Saunders**, and twelve first-place winners of Metropolitan Opera auditions.

Pilla's career as one of the great sopranos of the 1920s was subsidized by her supportive but strict Italian-American family, though her father required a little convincing at first. Just as she was completing high school, Pilla attracted the attention of **Agide Jacchia**, then director of the Conservatory and conductor of the Boston Pops Orchestra. "By that time, my father was beginning to give in to all of these people who were telling him, 'Pilla,

you can't hold your daughter back. She's got to be allowed to sing.'" Eventually, it became clear to her father and everyone who knew her that Pilla was bound for greatness—and she did not disappoint. Her grandmother later sold the family's longtime three-decker home in Lynn, Massachusetts to pay for travel expenses so that Pilla could tour Europe. She was well received in Italy, where she had a brief but spectacular run, and it was a great source of pride to her family that she had the chance to study opera and perform on some of the world's greatest stages.

Pilla spent the rest of her life teaching, and coached her last student in her home at Goddard House in Jamaica Plain, Massachusetts, just one day before her death in March 1997 at the age of 92.

Lorraine Hunt Lieberson

"When **Lorraine Hunt Lieberson** sang, time itself stopped to listen," wrote *The Boston Globe*'s classical music critic **Richard Dyer** in the obituary for the famed opera singer, who died on July 3, 2006 at the age of 52 from complications from breast cancer.

A mezzo-soprano whose voice inspired awe in those fortunate enough to have heard her sing, Hunt Lieberson performed until shortly before her death. "She was the most remarkable singer I ever heard. She was incapable of giving a routine performance," wrote **Alex Ross** in *The New Yorker*. "Each appearance had something explosively distinctive about it—and her career took the form of a continuous ascent."

Hunt Lieberson was born in San Francisco to parents who were active in the opera and music communities, but only began singing earnestly at the age of 26, after she enrolled at the Conservatory to study viola. She first sang professionally in 1984 with the Cantata Singers in a concert performance of Mozart's opera *Il re pastore*. For that concert, she billed herself as a soprano, but later found her "viola voice," she told *The Boston Globe*. From Boston, her career took her all over the world to perform with great orchestras and opera companies, but she regularly returned to the city where it all began.

Her husband, the late composer **Peter Lieberson** (1946–2011), wrote that her style transformed the way he composed. In 2005, she performed his *Neruda Songs* with the Boston Symphony Orchestra (BSO) at Symphony Hall, and then returned in early 2006 to sing his *Gurrelieder*.

Hunt Leiberson won two Grammy Awards posthumously. She received the 2007 Grammy Award for Best Classical Vocal Performance for *Rilke Songs*, which was written by her husband, and a 2008 Grammy Award for her recording of *Neruda Songs*, also composed by her husband.

The McCloskys

After retiring from Boston University in 1967, classical baritone **David Blair McClosky** joined the faculty of Boston Conservatory of Music, where he established the graduate training program in voice therapy. He was joined by his wife, **Barbara McClosky**, also a voice teacher, in 1974.

McClosky was the son of two professional singers and came to Boston to train at the New England Conservatory, graduating in 1925. McClosky and Barbara were married in 1944 and moved to Duxbury, Massachusetts. There, "they taught privately for many years, working with a range of singers," recalled **Deborah Bennett Elfers**, a Boston arts philanthropist who trained with the McCloskys as a teenager.

McClosky enjoyed a successful performing career while teaching, including more than twenty solo performances with the Boston Symphony Orchestra. McClosky recalled, many years later, that while nursing a vocal injury in 1946, he developed some "light vocal techniques" that allowed him to perform just two weeks later. What would have seemed an unfortunate occurrence eventually led him to his second—and some say more important—career as a vocal therapist, even developing his own vocal technique. Among his many vocal coaching clients was **John F. Kennedy**.

In 1984, Barbara cowrote a book with her husband, titled *Voice in Song and Speech*. David McClosky died in September 1988 at the age of 85. Barbara died on March 18, 2015 at the age of 97. The couple's many former students mourned their passing.

The McCloskys practicing an aria in their studio at the Plymouth Rock Center, July 1950.

Words from Willa Cather

At the dawn of the twentieth century, Boston Conservatory was known for fostering musical talent regardless of gender, race, or social standing. These values are evident in **Willa Cather**'s short story, "A Wagner Matinee."

First published in 1905 as part of Cather's short story collection, *The Troll Garden*, "A Wagner Matinee" tells the story of the narrator's Aunt Georgina, an older, world-weary woman who "had been a music teacher at the Boston Conservatory, somewhere back in the latter Sixties." Years after the woman gave up music for life on a Nebraska farm, she visits Boston and attends a Symphony Hall concert with her nephew. The afternoon concert rejuvenates her and immediately washes away years of a hard and oppressive rural life.

"The first number was the *Tannhäuser* overture," Cather writes. "When the horns drew out the first strain of the *Pilgrim's Chorus*, Aunt Georgina clutched my coat sleeve. Then it was I first realized that for her this broke a silence of thirty years."

Cather, who was raised in Nebraska, was familiar with Boston and New England. She had no known connection to the Conservatory, but was an opera devotee until her death in 1947. Today a highly celebrated author, Cather's tie to the Conservatory is a treasured nod to the school's long-lasting legacy.

A Wagner Matinée

By WILLA SIBERT CATHER

I RECEIVED one morning a letter written in pale ink, on glassy, blue-lined note-paper, and bearing the postmark of a little Nebraska village. This communication, worn and rubbed, looking as though if had been carried for some days in a coat-pocket that was none too clean, was from my Uncle Howard. It informed me that his wife had been left a small legacy by a bachelor relative who had recently died, and that it had become necessary for her to come to Boston to attend to the settling of the estate. He requested me to meet her at the station, and render her whatever services might prove necessary. On examining the date indicated as that of her arrival, I found it no later than to-morrow. He had characteristically delayed writing until, had I been away from home for a day, I must have missed the good woman altogether.

The name of my Aunt Georgiana called up not alone her own figure, at once pathetic and grotesque, but opened before my feet a gulf of recollections so wide and deep that, as the letter dropped from my hand, I felt suddenly a stranger to all the present conditions of my existence, wholly ill at ease and out of place amid the surroundings of my study. I became, in short, the gangling farmer-boy my aunt had known, scourged with chilblains and bashfulness, my hands cracked and raw from the corn-husking. I felt the knuckles of my thumb tentatively, as though they were raw again. I sat again before her parlor organ, thumbing the scales with my stiff, red hands, while she beside me made canvas mittens for the huskers.

The next morning, after preparing my landlady somewhat, I set out for the station. When the train arrived I had some difficulty in finding my aunt. She was the last of the passengers to alight, and when I got her into the carriage she looked not unlike one of those charred, smoked bodies that firemen lift from the *débris* of a burned building. She had come all the way in a day coach; her linen duster had become black with soot and her black bonnet gray with dust during the jour-

ney. When we arrived at my boarding-house the landlady put her to bed at once, and I did not see her again until the next morning.

Whatever shock Mrs. Springer experienced at my aunt's appearance she considerately concealed. Myself, I saw my aunt's mis-shapen figure with that feeling of awe and respect with which we behold explorers who have left their ears and fingers north of Franz Josef Land, or their health somewhere along the Upper Congo. My Aunt Georgiana had been a music-teacher at the Boston Conservatory, somewhere back in the latter sixties. One summer, which she had spent in the little village in the Green Mountains where her ancestors had dwelt for generations, she had kindled the callow fancy of the most idle and shiftless of all the village lads, and had conceived for this Howard Carpenter one of those absurd and extravagant passions which a handsome country boy of twenty-one sometimes inspires in a plain, angular, spectacled woman of thirty. When she returned to her duties in Boston, Howard followed her; and the upshot of this inexplicable infatuation was that she eloped with him, eluding the reproaches of her family and the criticism of her friends by going with him to the Nebraska frontier. Carpenter, who of course had no money, took a homestead in Red Willow County, fifty miles from the railroad. There they measured off their eighty acres by driving across the prairie in a wagon, to the wheel of which they had tied a red cotton handkerchief, and counting its revolutions. They built a dugout in the red hillside, one of those cave dwellings whose inmates usually reverted to the conditions of primitive savagery. Their water they got from the lagoons where the buffalo drank, and their slender stock of provisions was always at the mercy of bands of roving Indians. For thirty years my aunt had not been farther than fifty miles from the homestead.

But Mrs. Springer knew nothing of all this, and must have been considerably shocked at what was left of my kinswoman. Beneath

Boston Symphony Orchestra Connections

When Boston Pops Orchestra conductor **Agide Jacchia** assumed leadership of Boston Conservatory of Music in 1920, it deepened the connection that the school had with the Boston Symphony Orchestra (BSO), which is traced back to the orchestra's founding in 1881.

Jacchia, who came to Boston in 1918 to conduct the Pops, was known for collaborations that brought together the city's artists, including hiring musicians from the BSO and the Pops to teach at the Conservatory.

Perhaps most notably, Jacchia brought a young **Arthur Fiedler** to teach harmony and viola at the Conservatory for a few years starting in 1920. About twenty years later, Fiedler, who by then was the Pops conductor, saw **Jan Veen** dance in New York City and invited him to come to Boston to perform with the Pops. That relationship lasted more than ten seasons.

Conservatory President **Richard Ortner** also had ties to the BSO; he came to the school after a twenty-three-year career at the Tanglewood Music Center, which is the symphony's summer institute for advanced musical training.

The BSO has a long history of players who have been on the Conservatory's faculty and alumni who have performed with the orchestra. Those musicians, listed with their time at the BSO and their tenure at the Conservatory, include:

- **Eugene Adam**, trombone and tuba, 1917–1947, taught the same from 1920–1943
- **Raymond Allard**, bassoon 1922–1936, principal bassoon 1936–1953, taught same from 1933–1945
- **Emilio Arcieri**, E-flat clarinet, 1921–1934, percussion 1934–1949, taught clarinet from 1920–1950
- **Ronald Barron**, principal trombone 1975–2008, taught trombone from 1971–1977

- **Catherine J. Basrak**, assistant principal viola, Conservatory instructor
- **Augustus Battles**, flute and piccolo, 1909–1935, taught the same from 1921–1928
- **Albert Yves Bernard**, viola, 1925–1967, taught the same from 1948–1972
- **Gaston Bladet**, flute, 1923–1938, taught the same from 1933–1938
- **Norman Bolter**, trombone and euphonium, retired from the BSO in 2008, instructor
- **John Coffey**, trombone, 1941–1952, taught the same from 1964–1980
- **Geralyn Coticone**, piccolo, retired in 2003, instructor of piccolo and flute
- **Doriot Dwyer**, principal flute, 1952–1989, taught the same from approximately 1995–2015
- **Daniel Eisler**, violin, 1925–1950, taught the same from 1928–1950
- **Gaston Elcus**, violin from 1925–1952 and taught violin from 1933–1960
- **Ronald Feldman**, violin and assistant conductor, 1967–2001

- **Plácido Fiumaro**, second violin at the time of his death in 1917, was a student of **Julius Eichberg**

- **Henri Girard**, double bass from 1920–1966, taught the same from 1931–1967

- **Max Hobart**, violin/assistant concertmaster, 1965–1992, taught the same from 1968–1970 and 1978–1986

- **Mihail Jojatu**, fourth chair cello, studied at the Conservatory

- **Phillip Kaplan**, flute, 1939–1970, taught the same from 1978–1984

- **Marcel Lafosse**, flute, 1928–1958, taught the same from 1933–1960

- **Jacobus Langendoen**, cello from 1920–1962, taught same from 1933–1964

- **Jean Lefranc**, viola, 1925–1947, taught the same from 1933–1948

- **Luis Leguia**, cello, 1963–2007, taught the same from 1972–1981

- **Jean Lemaire**, double bass, 1926–1939, taught the same from 1933–1940

- **George Madsen**, flute/piccolo, 1935–1965, taught the same from 1938–1950

- **Patricia McCarthy**, assistant principal viola, 1979–1993, taught the same from 1987–2013

- **Osbourne McConathy**, horn, 1944–1966, taught the same from 1950–1981

- **Jonathan Miller**, cello since 1971, instructor of cello

- **James Orleans**, double bass, Conservatory '81, *magna cum laude* and Boston Conservatory Distinguished Alumni Award recipient

- **Toby Oft**, principal trombone, since 2008, taught the same from 2008–2010

- **Josef A. Orosz, Sr.**, assistant principal trombone, 1943–1970, instructor of trombone, brass, 1928–1964

- **James Pappousakis**, flute, 1937–1977, taught the same from 1950–1979

- **Richard Plaster**, bassoon, 1952–1992, taught the same from 1954–1987

- **Attilio Poto**, second clarinet, 1948–1950, instructor, 1950–1992

- **Arthur Press**, percussion, 1956–1992, taught the same from 1967–1990

- **Mike Roylance**, principal tuba, since 2003, taught the same from 2004–2006

- **Chester Schmitz**, tuba, 1966–2001, taught the same from 1983–1998

- **Alfred Schneider**, violin, 1955–1998, taught the same from 1968–unknown

- **Robert Sheena**, English horn since 1994, instructor of English horn and oboe

- **Tom Siders**, assistant principal/third trumpet, 2009–present, taught the same since 2011

- **Louis Speyer**, oboe and English horn, from 1919–1964, taught same from 1920–1978

- **Simon Sternburg**, percussion, 1922–1952, taught the same from 1933–1944 and 1952–1964

- **Larry Wolfe**, assistant principal bass, 1970 to present, taught the same from 1973–1974 and since 1987

- **Douglas Yeo**, bass trombone, 1985–2012, taught the same from 2003–2004

- **Owen Young**, cello, instructor

Arthur Fiedler

He is best known as the maestro who introduced the Boston Pops Orchestra to the world, but before he started his tenure with the celebrated ensemble, **Arthur Fiedler** taught at Boston Conservatory.

Born in Boston, the son of Boston Symphony Orchestra violinist Emanuel Fiedler, Fiedler was a member of the Conservatory faculty in the early 1920s, where he taught courses in harmony and viola. During the same period, he founded the Boston Sinfonietta, which gave free outdoor concerts in Boston parks and public spaces, an idea Fiedler would champion his entire life.

Fiedler took over as the eighteenth conductor of the Boston Pops in 1930, nearly four years after his friend and Boston Conservatory President **Agide Jacchia** had headed the same group. Fiedler would go on to conduct the Boston Pops for nearly fifty years, making countless television appearances, recording numerous works, and establishing the Boston Pops as "America's Orchestra" by beginning the annual tradition of a Fourth of July concert and fireworks on the Charles River Esplanade in Boston.

Charles O. Budden and Joseph Antonelli

Before the G.I. Bill was created to provide college tuition for servicemen returning from World War II, there was the United States Veterans' Bureau, which compensated soldiers and sailors who were injured in World War I as a way to provide rehabilitation and employment.

Two such heroes were **Charles O. Budden** of Arlington, Massachusetts and **Joseph Antonelli** of Newton, Massachusetts, whose tuition to attend the Conservatory was paid for by the United States government after they were wounded in battle while serving in France.

Prior to World War I, Budden was an organist at the Old North Church in Boston's North End neighborhood, and Antonelli, a tenor, had several performance credits, including Robert Planquette's comic opera, *Les Cloches de Corneville,* or The Chimes of Normandy.

On March 11, 1928, *The Boston Globe* reported in a section called "Drama, Music, Pictures" that, "After graduating from the Conservatory, the two men made great success on Broadway in an act called 'Harmonizing As You Like It.'"

After their stint on Broadway and in touring productions, Budden and Antonelli continued to perform in the Boston area, including a series of concerts in the late 1920s at the Boston Theatre, which, along with an adjacent fire station on Washington Street, was demolished in 1926 to make way for the Keith Memorial Theatre, later known as the Opera House.

Top right: The organ at the Old North Church; *Below:* Line outside Boston Theater in the late 1920s

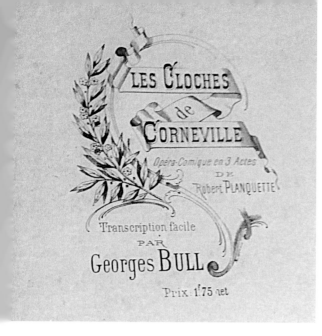

LES CLOCHES
de
CORNEVILLE

Opéra-Comique en 3 Actes
DE
Robert Planquette

Transcription facile
PAR
Georges BULL

Prix: 1f75 net

Albert Alphin

During his long leadership tenure, **Albert Alphin** expanded the Conservatory from a "small school of music" into an internationally recognized college of music, drama, and dance. Under his leadership, the Conservatory flourished, attracting a distinguished faculty, acquiring the majority of its current buildings and facilities, and obtaining the authority to grant degrees.

Born on a farm in Wolfscrape, North Carolina, Alphin came to Boston in 1920 to attend the Conservatory, where he studied composition with **Otto Straub**, organ with **Merton Frye**, piano with **George Vieh** and **Hans Ebell**, and conducting with **Agide Jacchia**. He was such a star pupil that after graduating in 1924, Jacchia invited him back to teach piano and solfeggio, which Alphin did until 1927.

In 1927, Alphin founded the National Associated Studios of Music (NASM), an organization that provided instructors for music programs. NASM offices were located on Huntington Avenue, just steps from the Conservatory.

After Jacchia's death in 1932, Alphin helped Jacchia's widow, **Ester Ferrabini Jacchia**, run the Conservatory. In 1933, they began discussions to formally transfer ownership of the school to Alphin and his company. That process of amalgamation was completed in late 1935, and NASM's board voted to change its name to Boston Conservatory of Music.

Upon assuming leadership of the Conservatory in 1936, Alphin began hiring a faculty of top-ranking instructors representing all corners of the city's artistic community. With a growing faculty, Alphin expanded class offerings to include dance and established a department for dance and drama, led by **Harlan F. Grant**.

Despite dire economic times in the 1930s, Alphin improved the Conservatory's financial situation and, in 1936, relocated the school from Huntington Avenue to a more spacious 26 Fenway. As enrollment increased over the next four years, Alphin purchased three additional buildings to use as dormitories.

In 1941, Alphin formally assumed the role of director of the Conservatory. From 1942 to 1943, he took a leave of absence to serve in the United States Army as conductor of the 301st Coast Artillery Corps Overseas Chorus. When he returned, he continued to expand course offerings and once again hired additional faculty and staff. In 1944, he married Conservatory alumna **Katherine M. Shepherd**, who taught solfeggio and piano at the school, and served as a house mother for the dorms along the Fenway.

An active artist and administrator, Alphin also served as choir conductor for the Greek cathedral in Boston and produced radio programs for Boston-area stations during his tenure at the Conservatory.

In 1949, Alphin finished a milestone project that he had begun more than a decade earlier: the construction of 31 Hemenway Street. Though Alphin had acquired the land and secured support to build this critical space from city agencies, banks, and donors, the project was delayed when the United States War Department denied the school access to the materials needed for construction. The project resumed after the war ended and the material ban was lifted.

Alphin continued in the role of director until his retirement in 1967. He remained involved with the Conservatory as the school's treasurer and was active on campus until his death on September 12, 1973, at the age of 72.

Alphin was a "humble man, never seeking personal glory or honor," Grant told *The Boston Globe* when Alphin died. "He was an untiring worker; the first to arrive and never leaving until the job was done."

The Albert Alphin Library at 8 Fenway is named in his honor—a leader who shaped the Conservatory into what it is today.

The First Major Faculty Expansion

When **Albert Alphin** began to take over the management of the Conservatory in 1933, his first priorities were to expand the faculty to include some of the most notable musicians and teachers of the day, and to broaden the range of course offerings beyond music instruction. To do this, he established an artistic board, just as he had in his National Associated Studios of Music (NASM), which operated as an agency employing private teachers in Boston and New York City. He brought in many NASM artists as a result.

Hans Ebell taught piano and harmony at the Conservatory, first under **Agide Jacchia** from 1920 to 1924 and then returning in 1933 from NASM at Alphin's invitation.

Conservatory students lined up for Ebell's classes, but he died in 1934—within just a year of joining the Conservatory—under suspicious circumstances that filled newspaper pages for more than a year afterward.

Alphin also invited theater professional **Harlan F. Grant** to make the transition from NASM to the Conservatory. Grant arrived at the school in 1933 and immediately launched what would later become the Drama Department. His courses in theater arts, art history, and drama were immensely popular, and he was a prominent figure on campus until he retired from teaching in 1977.

Nicolas Slonimsky, who taught piano and composition from 1933 to 1948, also joined the Conservatory from NASM. **Roger Sessions**, who knew Slonimsky in Europe, was advertised as a Conservatory teacher from 1933 to 1937. And, after touring Europe as an opera singer, alumna **Iride Pilla** returned to the Conservatory in 1936 as a member of the voice faculty.

Others who Alphin hired in his first years as director include:

Hugh Alexander, organ, 1937–1944
Raymond Allard, bassoon and saxophone, 1933–1945
Otto Asherman, dance, 1938–1944

Nicolas Slonimsky

Hans Ebell

Grace DeCarlton

Madeline Bernard, French, 1933
Gaston Bladet, flute, 1933–1938
J. Marcellin Cauhape, viola, 1933–1936
Margaret Chaloff, piano, 1933–1937
Trannie Yates Coburn Bouchard, piano,
    1938–1948
Oliver Daniel, piano, 1936–1938
Helen Maria Davis, psychology, 1933–1937
Grace DeCarlton, dance, 1933–1937
Lloyd Del Castillo, organ, 1933–1938
Marie DeMattheis, harp, 1933–1944
Harold Doyle, violin, string ensemble,
    1928, 1933–1977
Hippolyte Droeghmans, cello, 1933–1936
Gaston Eleus, violin, 1933–1960
Madge Fairfax, voice, 1936–1942

Elaine Fairfield, dance 1933–1936
Giorg Fior, piano, 1937–1957
Henri Girard, contrabass 1931–1933,
    1940–1967
Lucien Hansotte, trombone, 1938–1944
Caroline Hudson Alexander, voice,
    1937–1944
Hugo Kortschak, violin, 1933–1936
Jacobus Langendoen, cello, 1933–1964
Jean Lefranc, viola, 1933–1948
Jean Lemaire, contrabass, 1933–1940
Sidney Leonard, ballet, 1933–1950
George Madsen, flute, 1938–1950
Gino Umbarto Merluzzi, Italian, 1936–1944
Pearl Bates Morton, voice, 1934–1936,
    1938–1940

Frank Ramseyer, music history, 1934–1937
Irma Seydel, violin, solfeggio, 1920–1926,
    1933–1937 (also taught in Boston Public
    Schools)
Myrna Sharlow, voice, 1934–1940
Clara Shear, voice, 1933–1937
Wellington Smith, voice, 1933–1951
Simon Sternburg, percussion, 1933–1944,
    1952–1964
Laura Taylor, English, 1936–1938
Willem Valkenier, French horn, 1933–1950

Roger Sessions

After returning from music training in Europe in 1933, prestigious American composer **Roger Sessions** taught at the Conservatory for nearly five years. His arrival prompted Conservatory director **Albert Alphin** to take out newspaper ads announcing that Sessions had joined the faculty.

Despite his highly regarded reputation, accounts indicate that Sessions was slow to gather students during his first year. However, it was said that one young composer, **Alan Hovhaness**, was so intent on meeting Sessions at the Conservatory that he told Alphin he was a friend of Sessions in order to gain access. Hovhaness later recalled in an interview that the meeting had served as a catalyst for his own career as a composer and teacher at the Conservatory.

Sessions was born in Brooklyn, New York, into what he told *The New York Times* was a "very old American family." He was raised in New England and began his studies at Harvard College at the age of 14. After his time at the Conservatory, Sessions taught at Princeton University and the University of California at Berkeley, before returning to Princeton. He later won two Pulitzer Prizes, a special citation for his life's work in 1974, and the prize for music in 1982. After his retirement, Sessions taught at The Juilliard School until his death in 1985, at the age of 88.

Music historians, including Sessions' biographer **Andrea Olmstead**, have noted that it was during his time in the Northeast (he maintained homes in Boston, the Berkshires, and New York City) that Sessions honed the harmonic language for which history would remember him.

The Second Major Faculty Expansion

Like many other colleges and universities, Boston Conservatory of Music experienced an influx of students following World War II, in large part due to education subsidies financed by the G. I. Bill. The school's director, **Albert Alphin**, responded by bringing on yet another cadre of illustrious instructors.

One of the more notable faculty members to join the Conservatory during this time was Austrian-born pianist and composer **Karl Weigl**. Weigl had fled Austria with his wife, **Vally Weigl**, during the Nazi occupation, and like many other European wartime exiles, he became an American citizen. He arrived at the Conservatory in 1946 and stayed for nearly three years,

teaching music theory, composition, and conducting. He also taught in New York City for a short time before his passing in 1949 due to complications from cancer.

Other music luminaries who joined the faculty after World War II include: **Alan Hovhaness**, who taught composition from 1948 to 1951; **Hugo Norden**, who taught music theory, composition, violin, and counterpoint in two stretches at the Conservatory from 1944 to 1948 and 1976 to 1987; **Daniel Pinkham**, who taught harpsichord, analysis, music history, and composition from 1946 to 1962; and **Grace Hunter**, who provided voice instruction from 1946 to 1987.

Perhaps Alphin's most high-profile postwar recruit was **Jan Veen**, an internationally recognized dancer and dance instructor who moved his studio to the Conservatory in 1944 and taught dance and fine arts classes until his death in 1967.

Additional faculty hired in Alphin's post-1940 wave of expansion included:

Albert Yves Bernard, viola, 1948–1972
Emil Bouchard, voice, 1946
Isador Bouchard, voice, 1947–1949
Elford Caughey, harp, 1944–1950
Harry Cobel, dance, 1944–1948
Edgar Curtis, piano, organ, orchestra, 1947–1950

Alan Hovhaness

Hugo Norden

Karl Weigl

Joseph DePasquale, violin, viola, 1947

Walter Dole, flute, 1945–1954

Emmy Dortsak, piano, 1947–1958

Karl Geiringer, composition, theory, music history, 1944–1947

Albin Goldschmied, psychology, German, liberal arts, 1941–1946

Grace Warner Gulesian, piano, 1945–1963

Edmund Gurry, liberal arts, 1948–1950

David Holden, composition, theory, liberal arts, 1940–1944

Minna Franziska, piano, solfeggio, 1944–1951

Adele Hooper-Hugo, 1944–1958

Anne Kuhns, piano, 1948–1950

Wei-Ning Lee, piano, music theory, 1948–1965

Else Lewin, German, 1948–1950

Carl Ludwig, percussion, 1920–1934, 1944–1954

Osbourne McConathy, French horn, 1950–1981

Giuseppe Merlino, Italian, Spanish, 1946–1955

Camilla Tentera Molitore, voice, 1948–1954

Edward Molitore, voice, 1948–1954

Alfred Moseley, psychology, history of education, 1946–1947

R. Rice Nutting, theory, history of literature, 1944–1948

Grover Oberle, organ, church music, 1947–1959

Emanuel Ondricek, organ, 1948–1950

Jane Ragan, solfeggio, 1948–1951

Abbie Conley Rice, voice, 1948–1954

Rulon Robison, voice, 1946–1958

Harold Rubens, piano, 1944–1945

Benno Sachs, German, theory, 1948–1950

Anna Schmoyer, French, 1948–1950

Albert Sherman, theory, piano, music history, 1920–1922, 1946–1950

Marabelle Stebbins, solfeggio, 1947–1948

Donald Sullivan, voice, 1948–1952

Ludwig Theis, organ, 1944–1948

Burton Thiel, English, 1946–1948

Evelyn Thompson, piano, 1945–1947

Bedrich Vaska, cello, string ensemble, 1948–1954

Edith Vogl, piano, languages, fine arts, 1945–1946

Joseph Wolf, psychology, 1947–1950

Kappa Gamma Psi Fraternity

From the moment **Albert Alphin** arrived as a student at The Boston Conservatory and College of Oratory in 1920—the same year that **Agide Jacchia** took over the school—he never stopped working to increase the school's prestige.

In 1923, Alphin led the movement to launch the Gamma chapter of the Kappa Gamma Psi fraternity as a way to strengthen the relationship between faculty and students. It would serve as a recognized branch of a fraternity of the same name that was founded at New England Conservatory of Music in 1913.

Upon his graduation in 1924, Alphin continued to build the membership of the male-only organization, which by then was growing nationally with chapters at several colleges. This fraternity was founded after Phi Mu Alpha, the primary national music fraternity, which also was started at New England Conservatory of Music in 1898.

As president of the Conservatory's Kappa Gamma Psi chapter, Alphin organized a large program for the school's alumni on April 15, 1926 that was held at the Y-D Club at 200 Huntington Avenue. The evening's program included "Miss **Freda Berman** [who] entertained with a group of interesting dances including a ballet ... [and] vocal selections were by Miss **Rosalia Levy**."

The reception committee was made up of students, alumni, and faculty of the Conservatory, including Alphin, **G.T. Straub**, **John Leavitt**, and **Carl Peterson**. The dance committee was **Otto G. Straub**, **Armando Leuci**, **George Vieh**, **Joseph Orosz**, and **Joseph Healy**.

Κ Γ Υ

a Chapter

Conservatory of Music – 1925 – 1926.

Standing –

Adolfo M...

Albert De...

Carl Pete...

Joseph Va...

Harold D...

Joseph H...

Joseph On...

Kenith W...

Sitting –

Otto Str...

Albert Al...

John Lea...

George A...

Daniel R. Pinkham

Daniel R. Pinkham, renowned musician, composer, conductor, and sought-after teacher, was among the wave of distinguished instructors hired in the 1940s by Boston Conservatory of Music director **Albert Alphin**. A pioneer of Boston's early music movement, Pinkham taught harpsichord, analysis, music history, and composition at the Conservatory from 1946 to 1962. In 1958, Pinkham was named organist and musical director of the historic King's Chapel, an affiliation he would maintain for four decades.

A native of Lynn, Massachusetts, Pinkham began his music studies at the age of 5. He later studied composition with some of the most eminent composers of the twentieth century, including **Paul Hindemith**, **Arthur Honegger**, **Nadia Boulanger**, and **Samuel Barber**, with whom he studied at Tanglewood. Pinkham also took classes from **Aaron Copland** and **Walter Piston** at Harvard University, according to his obituary in *The Boston Globe*.

In addition to his work at the Conservatory, Pinkham taught at Boston University, Simmons College, and New England Conservatory of Music, where he was a faculty member from 1959 until his death in 2006 at the age of 83.

The Age of Jazz

Many notable Boston Conservatory alumni went on to make names for themselves in jazz, including saxophonist and bandleader **Sam Rivers**, guitarist and arranger **Turk Van Lake**, performer and educator **Makanda K. McIntyre**, **"Slam" Stewart**, **Don Redman**, **Gigi Gryce**, and **Michael Gibbs** (who also studied at Berklee College of Music and later taught the world-renowned vibraphonist **Gary Burton**), among others.

Rivers, who *The New York Times* called "an inexhaustibly creative saxophonist, flutist, bandleader and composer who cut his own path through the jazz world," enrolled at Boston Conservatory of Music in 1947, where he studied composition with **Alan Hovhaness** and later transferred to Boston University. Rivers' playing can be heard on more than fifty albums. He is also remembered for leading the 1970s free-jazz "loft scene" in New York.

Turk Van Lake maintained two careers. Born in Boston as Vanig Rupen Hovsepian and raised in New York, he studied 12-tone composition at the Conservatory. Using his birth name, he was a classical composer. Using his stage name, he was a jazz guitarist and arranger during the swing era. He also taught for many years at the College of Staten Island.

Born in Boston, **Makanda K. McIntyre** entered the Conservatory on the G.I. Bill and completed his master of music degree in composition in 1959, and a doctorate in education from the University of Massachusetts in 1975. McIntyre, who was known as Ken McIntyre until the 1990s, died in June 2001 at the age of 69. In his obituary, *The New York Times* wrote about McIntyre's best-known album, *Looking Ahead*, which was released in 1960 and featured McIntyre's compositions for saxophone, for which he played alto saxophone with saxophonist **Eric Dolphy**. McIntyre's unique style of playing, which was showcased on that album, resonated forty years later, according to the *Times*. "Though he stayed within the basic harmonies of a tune's given chords, his cantering delivery was charmingly eccentric," **Ben Batliff** wrote, "bursting with vocalist devices: harrumphs, swoons and chuckles."

Clockwise from top left: Gigi Gryce and his album, Rat Race Blues, *written by Noal Cohen and Michael Fitzgerald, October 2014; Slam Stewart; Don Redman; Sam Rivers; Makanda McIntyre and his album,* Looking Ahead

Rat Race Blues
THE MUSICAL LIFE OF GIGI GRYCE

LOOKING AHEAD
KEN McINTYRE with ERIC DOLPHY

Don Redman

In **Don Redman**'s induction into the West Virginia Music Hall of Fame, he was lauded as "the first great arranger in jazz history … [who] essentially invented the jazz-oriented big band with tight, innovative arrangements that also left room for solo improvisations."

Redman was born in 1900 in Piedmont, West Virginia into a musical family; his father was a music teacher and his mother, a singer. Redman showed immediate promise, learning to play the trumpet at the age of 3 and joining his first band at the age of 6. When he was 11, Redman entered Storer College, a historically black school in Harpers Ferry, West Virginia, where he mastered several instruments. Upon graduation in 1920, he came to Boston for "advanced studies" at The Boston Conservatory and College of Oratory.

After completing his education, Redman played as a member of **Billy Paige**'s Broadway Syncopators for a year. A talented alto saxophonist and clarinetist, Redman played sax on early recording sessions for **Duke Ellington**, **Ma Rainey**, **Bessie Smith**, **Ethel Waters**, and others.

He later earned a reputation as a music arranger. In the late 1920s, Redman was the chief arranger for **Fletcher Henderson**, who is widely recognized as one of the founders of the big band swing tradition. Redman also wrote for all-white bands (as they were called at the time) led by **Isham Jones**, **Ben Pollack**, and **Paul Whiteman**.

In the 1940s, Redman worked as a freelance arranger for radio shows and wrote for **Count Basie**, **Cab Calloway**, and **Jimmy Dorsey**. His all-star orchestra is credited as the first band from the United States to tour in post–World War II Europe. In later years, he was the arranger for the singer **Pearl Bailey** and led his band in her revues.

Redman died in 1964, but his family's musical tradition continues through his nephew, saxophonist **Dewey Redman**, and great-nephews, saxophonist **Joshua Redman** and trumpeter **Carlos Redman**.

Don Redman (center) and his orchestra, New York City

Leroy Eliot "Slam" Stewart

Leroy Eliot "Slam" Stewart may have only spent a short time at the Conservatory during the 1930s, but coming to Boston forever changed his career and influenced a generation of jazz musicians.

A native of Englewood, New Jersey, Stewart started playing the violin at the age of 6, but he turned his attention to string bass years later, telling interviewers that he "didn't care for the timbre of the violin." It was on the string bass that he made his name.

In 1934, Stewart "spent a year studying at [T]he Boston Conservatory and College of Oratory], where he heard a jazz violinist, **Ray Perry**, singing along with his solos," *The New York Times* wrote in Stewart's obituary on December 10, 1987. "[He] began singing along with his own bowed bass, but pitching his voice an octave higher, creating a broader, more sumptuous sound." While some critics of the day labeled Stewart's unique playing style a "gimmick," *The New York Times* wrote that he was highly sought after for his "more conventional bass-playing skills" and used his stylized method "in a musicianly fashion, for musical rather than novelty effects."

Slam Stewart died at the age of 73, after a successful career that included performing with a long list of jazz greats, including **Red Norvo, Teddy Wilson, Charlie Parker, Dizzy Gillespie, Beryl Booker, The Benny Goodman Sextet, Don Byas, Johnny Guarnieri, Art Tatum, Erroll Garner, Coleman Hawkins, Fats Waller,** and **Lester Young.**

Bottom: Slam Stewart and Slim Galliard, circa 1938

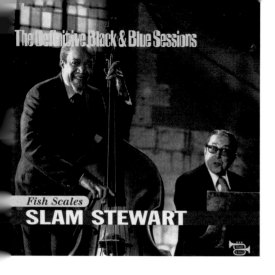

The Definitive Black & Blue Sessions

Fish Scales
SLAM STEWART

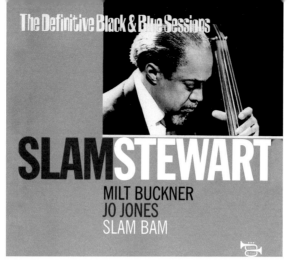

The Definitive Black & Blue Sessions

SLAM STEWART

MILT BUCKNER
JO JONES
SLAM BAM

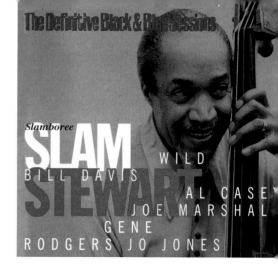

The Definitive Black & Blue Sessions

Slamboree
SLAM STEWART

WILD
BILL DAVIS
AL CASE
JOE MARSHAL
GENE
RODGERS JO JONES

Rhodes Composes New Symphony

William Andrew Rhodes, Mus. B., composer-music critic of Boston, Mass., has composed a new symphony in four movements, and named it "Glory Bound Symphony." According to Boston music critics, and music teachers who have analyzed the Symphony, it is said to be one of the finest Symphonies composed by a Race composer. Last season, Mr. Rhodes composed a Symphonic Composition, and gave it the title "Plantation Festival," which was played by the Boston Symphony Pops Orchestra of eighty-five musicians in Symphony Hall. He was presented to the large audience by Mr.

WM. H. RHODES
Distinguished Composer

Arthur Fiedler, who conducted the orchestra, and the audience gave Mr. Rhodes a big ovation. Mr. Warren Storey Smith, eminent music critic of the Boston Post Newspaper, also praised Mr. Rhodes highly.

The New England Conservatory of Music 1932 Endicot[t] Prize in Composition, and the Conservatory 1933 Edwin P. Brown Prize were awarded Mr. Rhodes. He also has the distinction of

CANDIDATES FOR THE CERTIFICATE

PALMA DENEAULT, *Pianoforte*
New Bedford, Massachusetts

CHARLOTTE GISELE DISCO, *Pianoforte*
Norwich, Connecticut

CANDIDATES FOR THE DEGREE OF BACHELOR OF MUSIC

HELEN ELIZABETH HORAN, *Voice*
Glenwood Springs, Colorado

WILLIAM ANDREW RHODES, *Composition*
Greensboro, North Carolina

KATHERINE MARY SHEPHERD, *Pianoforte*
Dedham, Massachusetts

PROGRAM

BRANDENBURG CONCERTO, No. 6................*J. S. Bach*
  allegro
      adagio
          allegro
              For String Orchestra
              DAVID HOLDEN, *Conductor*

ADDRESS
  REV. ARTHUR B. WHITNEY,
      Pastor, First Parish Church, Quincy, Mass.

ANNOUNCEMENT OF SPECIAL AWARDS
  GEORGE C. VIEH,
      Member, Board of Trustees and of Faculty

PRESENTATION OF THE CERTIFICATES AND DEGREES
  ALBERT ALPHIN,
      President, Board of Trustees

William Andrew Rhodes

When noted pianist, church organist, and composer **William Andrew Rhodes** graduated from Boston Conservatory of Music in 1940 with a bachelor of arts degree, it was the first time that an African American had received a degree in composition from a Boston institution.

Like so many students interested in studying music in Boston in the early twentieth century, Rhodes had sought out the Conservatory for his education.

Recognizing his promise as a talented artist, the Conservatory—led at the time by noted opera conductor and arranger **Agide Jacchia**—granted Rhodes a scholarship to study keyboard, harmony, and composition. As a student, the Greensboro, North Carolina native earned a reputation as a skilled composer. **Arthur Fiedler** and the Boston Pops Orchestra premiered Rhodes' internationally acclaimed *Glory Bound*

Symphony in 1940, just after he graduated from the Conservatory.

After his studies, Rhodes served as the organist and choir director of the Ebenezer Baptist Church in Boston's South End for many years. He also founded the Rhodes Opera Society in 1936, which toured for several years. Rhodes died in 1963 at age 58 in his home at 552 Massachusetts Avenue, Boston.

Gigi Gryce

Like so many who came to the Boston Conservatory, jazz saxophonist and composer **Gigi Gryce**'s training unlocked a whole new way of thinking and performing.

Gryce was born George General Grice, Jr., in Pensacola, Florida in 1925 and spent his childhood in Hartford, Connecticut. Despite showing some musical talent in high school, Gryce originally thought he would pursue a career as a physician. It was after being drafted in 1944 into the United States Navy that he met professional musicians **Clark Terry**, **Jimmy Nottingham**, and **Willie Smith**, who convinced Gryce to pursue a career as a musician, according to **David Griffith**, who maintains a website about Gryce.

After three years in the Navy, Gryce entered Boston Conservatory of Music on the G.I. Bill, where he was influenced and inspired by his teachers, organist and composer **Daniel Pinkham** and composer **Alan Hovhaness**, according to a biography on Gryce written by **Noal Cohen** and **Michael Fitzgerald**.

At the Conservatory, Gryce honed his chops on saxophone, clarinet, and flute, and he also arranged and composed music. A quiet, understated man, Gryce (who changed the spelling of his name for stage use) is credited with writing three symphonies, a ballet, and several other short pieces—all before he graduated in 1952 with a degree in composition.

In 1948, while he was a student at the Conservatory, Gryce was an arranger for jazz pianist and bandleader **Sabby Lewis** and had paying gigs with jazz pianist and arranger **Thelonious Monk** and bebop jazz trumpeter **Howard McGhee**. It was while performing at Symphony Hall that Gryce came to the attention of **Stan Getz**, who asked Gryce to arrange for him. "Getz subsequently recorded three Gryce originals: *Yvette*, *Wildwood* and *Mosquito Knees*," according to Griffith's website.

After graduation, Gryce went to New York City and within a year would have his charts recorded by **Max Roach** and his own septet, as well as by McGhee

and **Horace Silver**'s sextets. Famed music producer **Quincy Jones** suggested to bandleader **Lionel Hampton** that he should hire Gryce for a tour of the United States and Europe.

Gryce's formal training informed his later work in jazz, but—according to his biographers—Gryce strictly separated his work as a classical composer (chamber works, a symphonic tone-poem, and piano pieces for two and four hands) and the arranging and composition for jazz greats, such as Hampton and Getz.

In addition to his remarkable career as a composer and performer, Gryce was a fierce advocate of composers' and musicians' rights. In 1955, he started his own music publishing company, Melotone Music, to secure payment and credit for those who made music, according to a website on his life.

Gryce died on March 14, 1983 at the age of 57.

saying somethin'!

GIGI GRYCE QUINTET

new jazz 8230

the gigi gryce quintet

with richard williams

THE RAT RACE BLUES

Concert

Original Compositions by Members of the Composition Class
(Performed by Students of the Conservatory)

PROGRAM

Rumi .... Vanig Hovsepian
    Cantata for Soprano Solo, Alto Solo, Mixed Chorus, Clarinet,
    Bass Clarinet, Horn and Viola (Poem by Rumi)
      (a) Prelude and Chorus
      (b) Intrada Alto Solo and Chorus
      (c) Soprano Solo and Chorus
      (d) Fugue and Chorus

Two Pieces for Clarinets .... Joseph Williams

Theme and Five Variations for String Quartet .... Louis Manulla

Starvation (for Winds and Violins) .... George Grice

Four Dances (for 2 Clarinets and Piano) .... Robert Lalumiere

Variations .... John McLoughlin
    Madrigal for Mixed Chorus and 5 Trombones

Two Motets .... Lawrence Bardouille
      (a) Motet for Women's Chorus
      (b) Motet for Mixed Chorus

Allegro from Piano Sonata .... Lawrence Bardouille

Two Pieces from Suite "International" .... Lawrence Bardouille
    For Winds, Strings and Percussion
      (a) L'Espanol
      (b) Oriental

Sonata for Winds and Timpani .... Ernest Furtado
    Allegro—Andante—Allegro

H. Wilfred Churchill

H. Wilfred Churchill played every role possible at the Conservatory: student, teacher, accompanist, administrator, and benefactor. The renowned pianist and teacher also ensured that his legacy lived on by being the first person to bequeath his estate to the Conservatory. Since 1994, The Churchill Piano Prize has provided annual financial support to talented piano students who study at the school.

Churchill was born in Yarmouth, Nova Scotia, where he studied piano as a child. His teacher brought him to Boston when he was about 14 years old to study with **Hans Ebell**. Churchill enrolled in the Conservatory to concentrate on his piano studies and was awarded a diploma, signed by Ebell and Chairman of the Board of Directors **Alfred H. Meyer**, on June 15, 1935, for completion of the Pianoforte Instructors Course.

After the Massachusetts Legislature chartered the Conservatory as a "college of music" in 1938, Churchill became the first to graduate from it with a bachelor of music degree, which was signed by Alphin and Meyer, and awarded on June 18, 1938. Churchill's diplomas hung outside Conservatory President **Richard Ortner**'s office at 8 Fenway for many years.

"The student body was very small, much like a family," Churchill said of his early days at the Conservatory. "Well, it's like a family now, in a way. But it really was then," Churchill said in the program for the school's 125th anniversary celebration.

Churchill began teaching while completing his bachelor of music degree, first under Ebell and later with **Heinrich Gebhard**, whose students included **Leonard Bernstein** and **Alan Hovhannes**. His teaching career lasted for more than forty years before he retired in 1977. He then worked another ten years as director of the Conservatory's Extension Division, retiring in 1987. He returned to campus to participate in the school's 125th anniversary events and was a presence at the school until his death in December 1992 at the age of 83. Today, his legacy lives on through scholarship and the giving society that bears his name.

The Boston Conservatory Campus

At its founding, Boston Conservatory of Music was located at Tremont Street, in what is now known as Boston's Theater District. Over the next several years, leadership changes and institutional growth led to a number of shifts in the campus location.

When **Agide Jacchia** took the reigns in 1920, he moved the school to Huntington Avenue, a move that reflected a blossoming of the city's arts scene, as several other major arts organizations had also recently moved to Huntington Avenue, according to **Anthony Pangaro**, a longtime Conservatory trustee who continues to serve on Berklee's Board of Trustees. Nearby, Symphony Hall had been constructed at 301 Massachusetts Avenue in 1900; Jordan Hall was built in 1903; and the Museum of Fine Arts moved to its home at 465 Huntington in 1909.

In 1936, **Albert Alphin** moved the Conservatory to the Fenway, the neighborhood that it has since called home. It was a move of necessity, as the growing school had new programs that needed a different kind of space, including dance rehearsal rooms. Alphin bought a total of six buildings along the Fenway, five of which are now historic brownstone residence halls. He also built and expanded 31 Hemenway Street.

As the school continued to grow, it looked at a number of space solutions, including attempts to rent space and purchase new buildings. For example, In April 1986, *The Boston Globe* reported that the Archdiocese of Boston rejected the Conservatory's bid to buy the Nazareth School on Pond Street in Jamaica Plain. "We're really bursting at the seams up here on the Fenway," **Curtis Hammar**, who was

then the Conservatory's spokesman, said of the school's seven-building campus. Because the school had more than 400 students at the time and was seeing a steady increase in enrollment, the trustees also looked at some empty buildings on the Andover, Massachusetts campus of Phillips Academy, but ultimately decided to stay in Boston. Over the lifespan of the Conservatory, various rented spaces also were leased to accommodate auxiliary services, classrooms, and archival space, including: 1161 Boylston Street, 72 Hemenway Street, and 6 Charlesgate West.

In 2013, the campus seemed complete with the new construction at 132 Ipswich Street, which provided a space large enough for a full orchestra rehearsal, more student practice rooms, and additional dance studio space. Then, in 2016, the

132 Ipswich Street

merger of The Boston Conservatory and Berklee combined the two campuses and once again expanded the Conservatory's footprint.

"There isn't any mistaking the school's presence today," Pangaro said.

154 Tremont Street: Situated across the street from the Boston Common, Julius Eichberg rented the back part of the fourth floor of 154 Tremont Street, which stood five stories tall. 154 Tremont Street—and the attached 155 Tremont Street—housed a number of notable businesses, including Mason and Hamlin Pianos, Mason Brothers Publishing, and R. Marriner Floyd, the jeweler, silversmith, and a musical instrument dealer who would later assume control of the Conservatory from the Eichberg family. 154 Tremont Street was designed by noted Boston

architect Charles Bullfinch as part of Colonnade Row. It was just a few blocks down the street from the Boston Music Hall—now the Orpheum Theatre—which was the original home of the Boston Symphony Orchestra.

515 Tremont Street: By 1901, the Conservatory—then led by R. Marriner Floyd—had moved to offices in the Odd Fellows Hall at 515 Tremont Street, located at the corner of Tremont and Berkeley. The school presented concerts on the building's main floor.

250 Huntington Avenue: When Agide Jacchia, then conductor of the Boston Pops Orchestra, took over the Conservatory in 1920, he set up shop at 250 Huntington Avenue, across the street from Symphony Hall. This was the Conservatory's location when Iride Pilla and Albert Alphin first

arrived as students; it was also famous for Ann's Restaurant, which was on street level until 1999. It was Betty's Wok & Noodle for a number of years and, by 2015, the Ginger Exchange Fresh Asian Kitchen.

256 Huntington Avenue: Agide Jacchia relocated the Conservatory to accommodate the school's growing need for space, this time just a few doors up Huntington Avenue at building number 256. It is from these offices that Ester Ferrabini Jacchia transferred ownership of the school to Albert Alphin in 1935.

236 Huntington Avenue: 236 Huntington Avenue housed Albert Alphin's offices for the National Associated Studios of Music (NASM), which he started in 1927 after resigning from his teaching position at the Conservatory. NASM employed a host of music instructors who gave private

31 Hemenway, circa 1959

8 Fenway, formerly the Boston Medical Library, became the centerpeice of the campus.

lessons, many of whom followed him to the Conservatory in 1933.

295 Huntington Avenue: The third and fourth floors of 295 Huntington Avenue housed Jan Veen's private dance studios, the Jan Veen Dance Studios. After a fire destroyed the building on May 19, 1943, Veen—who had a long history of working with Albert Alphin and the Conservatory—reestablished his private studio at Boston Conservatory, and later billed it as the Boston Dance Theatre.

26 Fenway: Albert Alphin and the Conservatory's board entered into a purchase-and-sale agreement for 26 Fenway on July 15, 1936. This marked the start of the school's move to the Fenway thoroughfare, although at the time, the city still called this area "the Back Bay." In September 1936, the first classes were held in 26 Fenway. In a 1943 review of

the Boston Conservatory String Quartet, *The Boston Globe*'s critic wrote of the performance space: "For one thing, the Concert Room of the Boston Conservatory is an admirable place in which to hear chamber music. Its acoustical properties are excellent. Furthermore, the sheer tonal beauty produced by this quartet in this resonant hall was glorious."

24 Fenway: Acquired in 1937, 24 Fenway allowed the school to accommodate its growing enrollment, which totaled 250 students who hailed from nearly every state in the United States and Europe. The 1940 United States Census records list 24 Fenway as the primary residence of Albert and Katherine M. Alphin, as well as piano instructor H. Wilfred Churchill.

32 Fenway: On August 24, 1938, Albert Alphin signed a deal to lease 32 Fenway as a dormitory, with an option to purchase

it. The board voted to buy the building on December 30, 1938. The loan was paid off on November 1, 1945.

40 Fenway: Albert Alphin signed the paperwork to purchase 40 Fenway on September 11, 1941, and the building was immediately used as a dormitory because of continued growth in student enrollment.

31 Hemenway Street: Albert Alphin's dream for the Conservatory was fully realized with the 1941 purchase of 31 Hemenway Street. The three-story building was planned to house the school's mainstage theater and rehearsal rooms. However, construction on the building was postponed until after World War II due to material shortage and did not officially begin until 1945. The building opened on April 17, 1949 with a celebratory concert featuring students and faculty. On October 15, 1958—nearly a decade later—the

Mayor Menino cutting ribbon for 132 Ipswich Street

Ipswich Street practice room

board approved a plan to borrow $60,000 to pay for the building's first renovation and expansion project.

27 Hemenway Street: The Conservatory bought a parking lot adjacent to its main classroom building on October 6, 2006, which allowed for the renovation and expansion of the adjacent building at 31 Hemenway Street. The project, which was completed in 2010, allowed for the creation of two performance spaces—Boston Conservatory Theater (325-seat mainstage venue) and Studio 401 (100-seat concert venue)—as well as classrooms, rehearsal spaces, dance studios, a designated box office, the Dance Division office, and the Theater Division office.

54 Fenway: On June 1, 1964, the school bought 54 Fenway, which sits at the edge of the campus in the Back Bay/

Fens. The school immediately began work to transform the building for use as a residence hall, but City of Boston inspectors issued a "notice-violation of law" for starting work on the bathrooms before the deed had been recorded.

8 Fenway: Less than two months after acquiring 54 Fenway, Albert Alphin and the board bought 8 Fenway, which at the time was the Boston Medical Library. After the purchase, 8 Fenway almost immediately became the Conservatory's centerpiece. As of 2017, the building features three performance spaces: Houston Hall (50 seats), Seully Hall (125 seats), and The Zack Box Theater (55 seats). It is also home to the Albert Alphin Library, the Boston Conservatory Welcome Center, an opera studio, classrooms, teaching studios, student practice rooms, a computer lab, and the Music Division office.

132 Ipswich Street: Not long after the 2010 renovation of 31 Hemenway Street, the Board of Trustees purchased a one-story building at 132 Ipswich Street. The original building was demolished in order for the Conservatory to design and construct a new building. The gleaming new building opened in 2014 and is home to teacher offices, dance studios, multipurpose studios, a performance library, the school's first-ever orchestra rehearsal hall, and professionally soundproofed practice rooms.

1 8 FENWAY	**8** 236 HUNTINGTON AVENUE
2 24 FENWAY	**9** 250 HUNTINGTON AVENUE
3 26 FENWAY	**10** 296 HUNTINGTON AVENUE
4 32 FENWAY	**11** 132 IPSWICH STREET
5 40 FENWAY	**12** 154 TREMONT STREET
6 54 FENWAY	**13** 515 TREMONT STREET
7 31 HEMENWAY STREET	

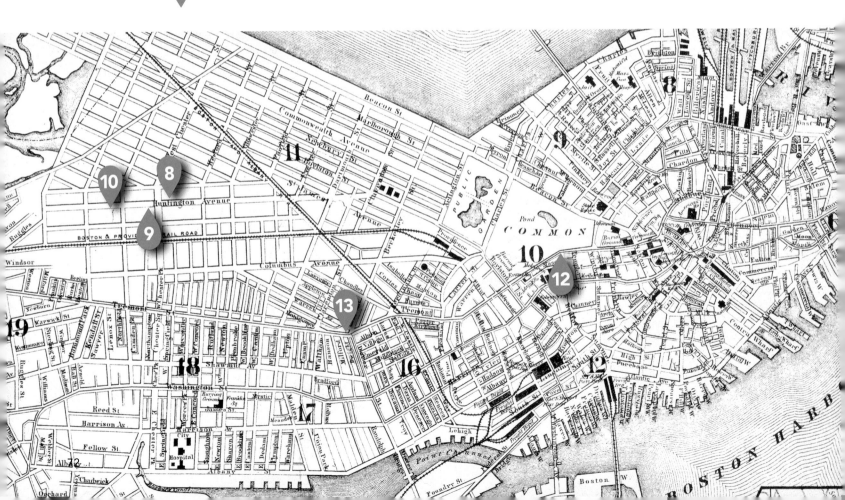

The Age of Dance and Theater

For many years, Boston Conservatory was first and foremost a violin school. While later expanding into cornet, voice, and other areas, it remained primarily a school of music until the 1930s and 1940s. At that point in the school's history, **Albert Alphin** hired **Harlan F. Grant** to teach drama, and he hired **Grace DeCarlton** and others to offer auxiliary courses in dance.

Alphin wanted to keep pace with similar schools, and tried to lure dancer **Jan Veen** to join the Conservatory as well. In 1943, Veen fell into misfortune when his private dance studio burned down, forcing him to take up residence at the Conservatory. Veen transformed the Conservatory's existing program into a degree-granting program. It was the first program in the United States to teach modern dance, as well as ballet.

Cordially
IanVeen

Harlan F. Grant

In the 1930s, **Harlan F. Grant** laid the foundation upon which the Conservatory's theater and musical theater programs were built.

Grant, like many others, followed **Albert Alphin** from his National Associated Studios of Music to the Conservatory when Alphin took over management of the school in 1933. (He even served on Alphin's artistic board of advisers and later the Conservatory's Board of Trustees.)

Grant founded the Drama Department at a time when Alphin was bringing on staff and expanding course offerings to make the school competitive with other programs in the city. This was particularly true for theater and dance.

Even when the Drama Department had only two instructors—including Grant—the course offerings and the training were broad and based on a classical structure. "Harlan was teaching, of course," **Robert Leibacher** said in a program note from the school's 125th celebration. "He was teaching things like 'History of Theater' and acting courses. That was my beginning at the Boston Conservatory," said Leibacher, who joined the faculty in 1963, teaching courses in English composition and literature. (Leibacher would remain on the faculty through 1992, teaching courses that included speech, acting, directing, and professional theater.)

In 1937, Grant started a summer stock season at the then-new Weston Playhouse Theatre Company in Weston, Vermont,

directing a production that featured a young actor named **Lloyd Bridges**. Grant hired a number of his Conservatory students and faculty to work at the Weston Playhouse over the years. Newspapers chronicled productions that Grant directed in Vermont and Boston, including new works by **Arthur Miller** and **Tennessee Williams**.

Mr. Grant, as he was known by students and colleagues alike, brought some of that "summer stock" feel to the Conservatory campus, remembers **Bob Monica** (B.F.A. '71, musical theater) through the "major musical production each year and he directed it."

Even though Grant and his contemporary in dance **Jan Veen** incorporated music

theater and dance productions into the curriculum as early as the 1930s, the first documented degree listing musical theater did not come until 1960, when student **Natalie Helms** graduated with a B.F.A. in drama, with a minor in musical theater. This continued to be the norm until later in the 1980s, when the musical theater program fully replaced the Drama Department. The Conservatory's graduates were working in musical theater even as the major developed, including two-time Tony Award–winner **Thommie Walsh**, who was listed as a dance major in the late 1960s and made history in the original cast of *A Chorus Line*.

Even though Grant stood only about 5'5" tall, he had a commanding presence. "Mr. Grant smoked a pipe, which he carried at all times, gesturing with it for emphasis," wrote Monica, who added that Grant always made sure to teach the Acting 101 class to first-year students. "Although Mr. Grant was at once commanding and perhaps a tad aloof, he could also be quite funny. His classes were as entertaining as they were informational, providing great insight into the art and technique of acting and directing. […] Harlan Grant was a superb teacher, director, and coach," Monica wrote. "I was fortunate … to learn from him during the years I spent [at the Conservatory]. [. . .] [T]he lessons he taught have stayed with me always."

Grant's wife, **Florence J. (Steele) Grant**, also worked at the Conservatory, teaching courses in stage makeup from 1950 to 1977. She and the couple's daughter, **Glenne Grant**, and the family's dog, a German shepherd named Fritz, regularly visited the campus and stopped by at the end of classes.

Grant led the department for decades and continued to teach until his retirement in 1977. He died on May 26, 1985 at the age of 78. Like Conservatory founder **Julius Eichberg**, Grant is buried at Mount Auburn Cemetery in Massachusetts.

Sue Ronson Levy

One thing that **Sue Ronson Levy**'s former Boston Conservatory colleagues remember about her is that she could talk faster than she could tap—and she had very fast footwork.

Ronson was a member of the faculty from 1979 until her retirement in 2001, and is credited with creating the school's tap program. An instructor of tap, Ronson's influence extended to students beyond the Dance Division. "She also regularly taught other faculty, and she, in turn, continued to take classes to hone her skills," said **Neil Donohoe**, the Conservatory's dean of theater, explaining that Ronson studied and achieved proficiency in many forms of dance, including Afro-Cuban jazz, jazz, ballet, ballroom, and improvisational dance.

Born Susan Aronson in the Coney Island section of Brooklyn, New York, Ronson dropped the first letter of her last name and was known professionally as Sue Ronson. She met her husband, **Norton A. Levy**, while she was leading dance classes in the Catskills. "I was her worst student, and she acted so nice to me, and we went out a couple of times," Levy told *The Boston Globe* for her obituary following her passing at age 75 in 2006. "She came to visit my mother in Boston, and before you know it, we were engaged and married."

Known for her expertise in "hoofing-style" tap in vaudeville parlance, Ronson began her dance career when, as a diaper-clad toddler, she wandered into a dance studio downstairs from her parents' apartment. Vaudeville appearances soon followed, and her first professional gig occurred when

she was just 4 years old, cast as Broadway legend **Ethel Merman**'s daughter in *Annie Get Your Gun*. Other musicals she performed in include *Carousel*, *Damn Yankees*, *Guys and Dolls*, and *Oklahoma!* As a teen, Ronson performed with **Sammy Davis Jr.**, **Burl Ives**, **Frank Sinatra**, **Paul Draper**, and **Larry Adler**, and when she was older, she traveled with **Bob Hope** on two overseas United States Organizations (USO) tours.

After her death, the Conservatory received many gifts in her honor, which allowed the school to create the **Sue Ronson Levy Scholarship** and provided financial support to dance students in 2007–2008 and 2008–2009. The Conservatory also formally changed the name of first-floor dance studio in 31 Hemenway to the Sue Ronson Tap Studio in her honor.

Ina Hahn

For many, the name **Ina Hahn** is synonymous with modern dance in Boston.

Hahn, who died on January 22, 2016 at the age of 86, had a long and distinguished teaching career, including her tenure at Boston Conservatory, where she taught modern dance, pedagogy, and repertoire from 1973 to 1977. Hahn also taught at Radcliffe College, Smith College, Boston Arts Academy, Northeastern University, Walnut Hill School, and Endicott College.

A Newton native and a graduate of Wellesley College, Hahn had a successful career on Broadway as a dancer. According to her obituary, "She appeared in the original 1950s Broadway productions of *Can-Can*, *The King and I*, and *Plain and Fancy*, working with the choreographers **Michael Kidd**, **Jerome Robbins**, **Helen Tamiris**, and **Agnes DeMille**. Originally an understudy for **Gwen Verdon** in *Can-Can*, she replaced Gwen, and Ina became a Broadway star overnight."

In 1968 Hahn and her husband, **Herbert Hahn**, bought what was reported to be the last working farm on Cape Ann and turned it into the Windhover Center for the Performing Arts. In June 2016, supporters gathered for a memorial fundraiser in Hahn's name to raise money for the center.

Thommie Walsh

A "dance maker," as *The New York Times* called him, Broadway dancer, director, choreographer, and Tony Award–winner **Thommie Walsh** was known during his time at Boston Conservatory of Music for his love of dance and an exuberance that went well beyond the stage.

"The first time I ever laid eyes on Thommie was in September 1968. [. . .] I had just completed a ballet class and was exiting the locker room when I heard the sound of loud, raucous laughter emanating from a dance studio," said Conservatory alumnus **Bob Monica** (B.F.A. '71, musical theater).

"When I peeked in, there was Thommie, dancing jubilantly around the room. [. . .] At first, I thought he was totally out of control; but I quickly understood that this was an amazingly talented and skilled dancer just free-styling a complicated and challenging dance routine. And he was performing for no other reason than the joy of expression."

Walsh was best known for his 1980s collaborations with **Tommy Tune** on the Broadway productions of *A Day in Hollywood/A Night in the Ukraine* and *My One and Only*, which earned them

two Tony Awards and four nominations. But it was Walsh's work in creating the role of Bobby in *A Chorus Line* that secured his place in Broadway history. Walsh modeled Bobby on his own story at the Conservatory, where he performed in several shows—including the school's 1969 production of *Carnival*—and was greatly influenced by his teachers **Ruth Sandholm Ambrose**, **Robert C. Gilman**, **Harlan Grant**, and **Robert Leibacher**.

Walsh passed away on June 16, 2007 at his family's home in Auburn, New York at the age of 57 from complications of lymphoma.

Top left: Cover art for Walsh's cassette, *Give My Regards to Broadway;*
Bottom: Walsh, at left, in the Conservatory's production of *Carnival*, 1968

"GIVE MY REGARDS TO BROADWAY"
THOMMIE WALSH

★ 1. GIVE MY REGARDS TO BROADWAY
★ 2. ALL ABOARD FOR BROADWAY
★ 3. TURN ME LOOSE ON BROADWAY
★ 4. PLEASE DON'T MONKEY AROUND
      WITH BROADWAY
★ 5. BROADWAY / LULLABY OF BROADWAY
★ 6. CARAVAN
  7. INDIAN DANCE
  8. BUCK DANCE
  9. HAPPY DANCING
 10. DANCING IN THE DARK

★ ON DanceVideo DV-4540

John Outlaw

John Outlaw, an actor and musician whose given name was Savage, hailed from Methuen, Massachusetts. He received a B.F.A. in musical theater from Boston Conservatory of Music in 1977. In 1987, Outlaw formed a rock band, the John Outlaw Project, and led as its singer and guitarist. He wrote songs about his battle against AIDS, which the group performed in clubs in Manhattan, where Outlaw lived at the time. Outlaw's "Down at the Drugstore," recorded in 1990, was made into a music video that aired on MTV.

Outlaw "had fought AIDS since 1979 and used [his] songs to dramatize issues about the epidemic." He died of the disease in March 1993 at the age of 37, according to his *New York Times* obituary. At the time of this death, he was one of the longest known survivors of AIDS, which in 1993 had no known treatment.

Outlaw's acting credits include numerous Off Broadway productions, several national commercials, and regular appearances on the soap operas *All My Children*, *Another World*, and *Guiding Light*.

"...Wow! I never liked the taste of other bran cereal. But Kellogg's® Cracklin' Bran® cereal has a rich, nut-like flavor that's really delicious."

Kellogg's
Cracklin'
bran

Jan Veen and the Dance Division

In 1943, **Jan Veen** and Boston Conservatory of Music entered a marriage of convenience that grew into one of the great love affairs in the school's history.

Veen was one of the city's most successful dancers, promoters, and teachers, and he believed that dance was for all. Through his eponymous school of dance on Huntington Avenue, Veen taught scores of children—from the gifted to those whose parents sent them to classes as recreation—as well as adult students. Veen also offered special classes for the so-called "older" students for Boston's Junior League and other civic organizations.

For years, Veen, who was active on the local music and performance scene, resisted the entreaties of Conservatory director **Albert Alphin** to take over the school's modest dance program that had been informally started in 1933 by **Grace DeCarlton**. But that all changed in 1943, when Veen's studio was gutted by a fire.

With a thriving school and a sudden need for studio space, Veen took Alphin up on his offer, but with some restrictions: the school would keep Veen's name and young students would be allowed on the

Conservatory's campus to take classes. (**Ruth Sandholm Ambrose**, who would teach under Veen and later run the dance program, would recall many years later that she missed the very young students and their energy.)

Born in 1903 in Vienna, Austria, Veen trained in modern dance with **Rudolf von Laban**, with expressionist dance pioneer **Mary Wigman** and others, before embarking on a touring career with several companies that took him all over the world. Veen first came to Boston at the invitation of Boston Pops maestro **Arthur Fiedler**, who had seen Veen perform in New York City.

From 1931 to 1941, Veen created thirty-seven original ballets for Fiedler and the Pops, including **Joseph Wagner**'s *Hudson River Legend* and **Walter Priston**'s *The Incredible Flutist.*

Veen's work at the Conservatory became formalized in 1943, when "he organized the first complete department of dance at the college level in the country," according to **Andrea Olmstead**, former chair of the school's Music History Department. In her 1985 independent research paper on the school's history, Olmstead writes that this

expansion came as part of Alphin's efforts to grow the Conservatory's offerings.

Veen believed that the school should do more in the realm of dance theater and music theater. In a 1949 interview with *The Boston Globe's* renowned music critic **Cyrus Durgin**, Veen spoke of "dance theater" and "music theater productions" and vowed to program whole seasons of musical and dance productions in the Conservatory's auditorium at the recently opened 31 Hemenway Street building. His first season kicked off with Indian musician **Wasantha Wana Singh** and a dance troupe, which was followed by a half dozen such concerts. Each visiting act also conducted master classes for students while on campus. This set the stage for the future musical theater degree and a new model for guest artists.

Veen died in June 1967 at the age of 62 after a long illness, according to *The Boston Globe.* His legacy in dance history was affirmed through his work at the Conservatory. It lives on through a scholarship given in his name each year to a deserving dance student.

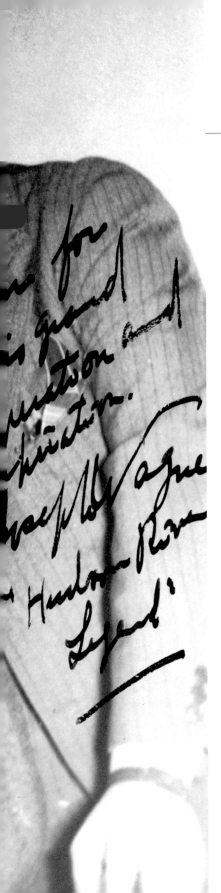

Hudson River Legend

When *Hudson River Legend*, a ballet based on the Washington Irving's *The Legend of Sleepy Hollow*, had its world premiere on March 1, 1944 at Jordan Hall in Boston, it featured a number of Boston Conservatory of Music students, staff, and alumni. This photograph was taken during a rehearsal of the 30-minute piece. It is inscribed by *Hudson River Legend* composer **Joseph Wagner** (standing right) to dancer and choreographer **Jan Veen** (standing left), who choreographed the ballet and trained the dancers from his studios at

the Conservatory. Wagner and Veen premiered the ballet with the Boston Civic Symphony, with **Arthur Fiedler** (seated) conducting. When the work was brought to the Conservatory, it was paired with another ballet by **Alan Hovhaness**, who taught composition at the Conservatory in the late 1940s and early 1950s and served as conductor for both works. For the premiere of *Hudson River Legend*, however, Hovhaness was in the orchestra, as the ballet's first performances were conducted by Fiedler.

Boston Ballet Connections

From the founding of the Boston Ballet in 1963, the city's premier professional company had a connection to Boston Conservatory and its instructors.

Jan Veen, who by the 1960s had gained an international reputation as the head of the Conservatory's Dance Division, collaborated with the company's founder **E. Virginia Williams** in "building the Boston Ballet," according to his obituary in 1967.

That support continued when **Ruth Sandholm Ambrose**, a classically trained ballerina, and **Robert C. Gilman** took over the Conservatory's Dance Department after Veen died.

Among the first Boston Ballet staff to join the faculty was **Anamarie Sarazin**, who had begun her twenty-year career with the ballet company in 1967 after two years of study at the Conservatory. When she suffered some health problems, Sarazin enlisted her Boston Ballet colleagues to teach her Conservatory classes, including: **Laura Young**, principal

dancer; **Mel Tomlinson**, a pioneering African American dancer who was a principal in Boston; the late **Sam Kurkjian**, former principal, ballet master, and the first resident choreographer at Boston Ballet; and soloist **Denise Pons Leone**, who continues to teach ballet at the Conservatory as of 2017.

Sarazin died in 1999 at the age of 53. In 2000, Sarazin's husband, **Al Petrucelli**, who was for many years the production manager of the Boston Ballet, established the Anamarie Sarazin Scholarship at the Conservatory in her memory. It is presented annually to an outstanding student of ballet entering his or her senior year.

Others from the Conservatory with Boston Ballet connections include: **Kristen Beckwith** (B.F.A. '64, dance), who teaches adult classes at the Ballet's Newton studio; **Naoko Harada Brown** (B.F.A. '02, dance), who teaches studio classes at the Ballet's Boston studio; **Sue Ronson Levy**, who taught tap at the Ballet's school; **Shannon McColl** (B.F.A. '13, dance), a Boston Ballet

former student who began teaching while studying at the Conservatory; **Clyde Nantais** (B.F.A. '73, dance), who began his association with the Ballet first as a dancer in 1973 and taught at the Conservatory from 1980 to 1989 and resumed teaching in 1991; and **Tommy Neblett**, the associate director of the Conservatory's Dance Division, who taught at the Ballet's Summer Dance Program.

Boston Ballet members continue to teach at the Conservatory, including former principal dancers **Adriana Suárez** and her husband, **Gianni Di Marco**, who in addition to teaching during the academic year were previously the artistic directors of The Boston Conservatory Summer Dance Intensive. Also, former Boston Ballet principal **Tai Jimenez** is on the Conservatory's dance faculty. She has several Broadway credits and some film roles to her credit in addition to her many notable ballet roles.

Top: Jan Veen and Ruth Sandholm Ambrose (center) perform in Boston Conservatory's *Dido and Aeneas*, 1959; *Bottom left:* Al Petrucelli and Anamarie Sarazin; *Bottom right:* Stephanie Dabney and Mel Tomlinson in Arthur Mitchell's "Manifestations," Dance Theater of Harlem, 1975

Ruth Sandholm Ambrose

Ruth Sandholm Ambrose was first a student at the Conservatory, but her long and heralded faculty career at the school officially began in May 1950, when Dance Division founder **Jan Veen** asked the celebrated ballerina to teach a class. The appointment was initially intended to last no more than a year, but Veen convinced Ambrose to stay on, which she did for more than forty years, teaching countless Conservatory dancers and sharing her passion for dance, first as an instructor and, later, after Veen died in 1967, as head of the Dance Division.

"Jan Veen had a huge morning class in which he combined students with his regular adult people—the Boston blue bloods and the Junior League, all kinds of people that had been following him through the years at his studio and at his performances

at The Boston Pops," Ambrose recalled in an article from the program for the Conservatory's 125th anniversary celebration. "I had first refused to come because I didn't think I would ever teach college. I had read that **Agnes DeMille** said that Boston was the worst dance town in the United States." Generations of Conservatory faculty and students are fortunate that Ambrose ignored DeMille, with whom Ambrose had studied.

Ambrose, who ran the Dance Division until 1989, also studied with **Lillian Cushing** and **Cia Toscanini**, and toured with **Adolph Bolm**'s ballet company. She was an actress with the Max Reinhart Touring Company and radio theaters in California and New York, and taught around the world. Throughout, the Conservatory

remained her home base and the place where she felt she had the greatest impact.

When word came in January 2015 that Ambrose had died in Florida, remembrances for the elegant dancer came pouring in, including from former President **William A. Seymour**, who called her "the Grande Dame of Dance at The Boston Conservatory."

"Mrs. Ambrose taught us to be lovers of dance—all dance—and to her, that meant lovers of storytelling," said **Michelle Chassé**, chair of musical theater dance and the first recipient of the Conservatory's Ruth Sandholm Ambrose Scholarship. "She respected work, but allowed you to play, knowing that the humanity was in the storytelling."

Dabney N. Montgomery

Selma, Alabama native **Dabney N. Montgomery** left his studies to serve in World War II as a member of the famed Tuskegee Airmen, and in 1951 enrolled at Boston Conservatory of Music to study ballet. During his time in Boston, he forged connections that would set the stage for a lifetime of devoted service to the community and to the arts.

When Montgomery returned from active duty in Italy, he first enrolled at Livingstone College in Salisbury, North Carolina. There, he joined the first intercollegiate black Greek fraternity, Alpha Phi Alpha, an affiliation that would later reinforce life-changing connections. While studying at the Conservatory a short time later, Montgomery also taught Sunday School, and through the church he met a woman who embraced him as her godson. One Sunday, she invited him to dinner to meet

her other godson—none other than fellow fraternity brother **Reverend Martin Luther King, Jr.**, who was studying in Boston University's doctoral program at the time. Montgomery also met King's fiancée, **Coretta Scott**, who was studying at the New England Conservatory. It was the first of several encounters he would have with Reverend King; in 1963, he marched under King's leadership at the March on Washington, and in 1965, he served as one of Dr. King's bodyguards on the historic march from Selma to Montgomery.

During his time at the Conservatory, Montgomery participated in several of **Jan Veen**'s productions before enrolling at the Metropolitan Opera School in New York, where an injury cut his dancing career short. He stayed in New York, however, living in Harlem and enjoying a long tenure in public service until his retirement from

the New York City Housing Authority in 1988. Throughout his sixty-two-year career, he volunteered actively at the Harlem YMCA and at his place of worship, Mother AME Zion Church, mentoring and developing leadership skills in the youth of Harlem.

Montgomery's life was a testament to Dr. King's dream. Devoted to the betterment of his community, he continued to work as a volunteer through 2015, and received awards and recognition from federal and state elected officials, as well as community and national organizations. Among the most notable was the Congressional Gold Medal of Honor bestowed upon the Tuskegee Airmen by President George W. Bush in 2007.

Montgomery died on September 3, 2016 at the age of 93.

Hugo F. Norden

Hugo F. Norden's long teaching career was bookended by engagements at the Conservatory, where his students remembered him as a nurturing instructor who pushed them to go places that they thought were out of reach. Composer **Jim Centorino** credited Norden with not only getting him into the Conservatory in the 1970s, but also with helping him graduate after only two years.

"He had a way of taking off his glasses, closing his eyes, and waxing philosophical," Centorino recalled of the influential instructor. "One time, he told me that 'The world is filled with mediocrity. All you have to do is sparkle a little and you will be lifted above that.'"

Norden, who taught at the Conservatory from 1944 to 1948 (and again from 1979 until his death in 1986 at the age of 76), taught composition, music theory, counterpoint, and violin. In addition to the Conservatory, Norden taught at Boston University and Boston College.

Born in Providence, Rhode Island, Norden began studying the violin at an early age and added music theory and composition to his studies at the age of 15. He later earned an undergraduate degree and a doctorate from the University of Toronto.

Attilio Poto

He was there for The Boston Conservatory's 125th anniversary, he was there for the opening of 31 Hemenway Street, and, most importantly, **Attilio Poto** was there for countless students throughout the forty-three years that he taught clarinet, sight-reading, and conducting—all mandatory subjects for those earning music degrees.

A native of Boston's North End, Poto took up the clarinet at age 11, and his musical talent soon landed him in a number of performing groups, including festival bands, a Works Progress Administration (WPA) orchestra, and a Boston youth orchestra that was conducted by **Fabien Sevitzky**, nephew of Boston Symphony Orchestra maestro **Serge Koussevitzky**.

After graduating from the city's English High School, Poto went to New York City for further study and served as the solo clarinetist for the Metropolitan Opera Company. In the late 1940s, he returned to Boston to perform in the clarinet section of the Boston Symphony Orchestra, under the direction of Koussevitzky and **Charles Munsch**, both of whom informed Poto's conducting style.

Poto's tenure with the Conservatory began in 1949, and he immediately made an impact on the school and his students. "In 1950, I studied clarinet with Attilio Poto and played under his baton in a Symphonic Band at [T]he Boston Conservatory," wrote **Anthony Morss** in a piece on the website Classical.net. "He also gave me a couple of lessons in conducting before I went to New York to study with one of his own teachers, **Leon Barzin**."

Morss, a conductor best known for his thirty-year-career as artistic director and principal conductor of Verismo Opera of Fort Lee, New Jersey, praised Poto for his teaching style and conducting technique: "Poto was a magnificent teacher: effective, demanding but warmly supportive. His crystal-clear and expressive baton technique made it a joy to play under his direction. After one professional concert he had conducted, I went backstage and asked some of the players, without revealing that I knew him, how they reacted to his conducting. They replied that they greatly appreciated his clarity, efficient musicianship, and even-tempered dignity."

Morss wrote that Poto is remembered for his appearance, "tall, slim, always quietly and impeccably dressed," and for using an unusually long baton—about three feet. A devoutly religious man, Poto filled his fourth-floor classroom with religious artifacts that reflected his deep faith as a Roman Catholic, including a statue of the Pope and the Virgin Mary.

In addition to serving as the conductor of the then-Boston Conservatory of Music Orchestra, Poto was named the conductor of the Harvard-Radcliffe Orchestra in 1954.

When he died on July 24, 2003 at the age of 88, Poto's neighbors in the North End remembered him as a man who deeply loved music and who had spent countless hours transferring stacks of reel-to-reel tapes and records to cassette tapes so that they could be enjoyed by modern audiences. His dedication to the arts and his students was evident throughout his life. "Every performance that went on at the Conservatory, every single performance, Mr. Poto was there," **James Bynum**, former director of financial aid, told *The Boston Globe* for Poto's obituary. "Anywhere there was good music, Mr. Poto would go."

Boston Conservatory's Centennial

When Boston Conservatory of Music celebrated its centennial with a concert featuring Conservatory students, faculty, and alumni on February 11, 1967, the spirit of the school's former director **Agide Jacchia** loomed large.

It was Jacchia, after all, who is credited with reviving the school when he took over in 1920. "The Conservatory of today is an extension of Jacchia's thinking," reporter **John Temple** wrote in an article about the school's centennial published on February 12, 1967, "and offers instruction throughout the areas of music, drama and dance."

At the time of the one hundredth anniversary, the Conservatory was led by Dean **George A. Brambilla** and Director **Albert Alphin**, and had 1,100 students, 500 of whom were enrolled full-time, according to the school's records. Alphin was a student of Jacchia's at the Conservatory and succeeded Jacchia's wife, **Ester Ferrabini**,

in running the school in 1933. Like Alphin, Jacchia had an immediate impact on the Conservatory. *The Boston Globe* observed in 1967 that Jacchia "changed the direction of the school more toward opera, whereas before his tenure it had emphasized instruction in string playing."

As *The Boston Globe* noted in its article on the centennial, "The Conservatory was the first of its kind in the United States, [with] the New England Conservatory opening one week later."

During the celebratory concert, Alphin and opera faculty member and alumna **Iride Pilla** honored the fifty-year teaching career of **Francis Findlay** by presenting him with a commemorative watch. At the time, Findlay was chairman of music education and graduate studies at the Conservatory, but his long teaching career also included a faculty position at New England Conservatory. Findlay died that December at the age of 72.

The Conservatory formally celebrated its one hundredth anniversary with a gala banquet in May 1967 at the Sheraton Hotel in Boston. According to a newspaper announcement of the fête, *Boston Globe* music critic **Michael Steinberg** was the evening's speaker, and **Mabel V. McKenney**, president of the Boston Conservatory Alumni Association, was the event's chairwoman.

The concert was given by the Boston Conservatory Orchestra with **Rouben Gregorian** conducting. It opened with Shostakovich's Festive Overture, op. 96, followed by two Verdi arias. McKenney ('64) sang "Ritorna Vincitor" from *Aida*, followed by **Evelyn Kazanjian**'s (B.M. '65, voice) performance of the aria "Ernani, involami" from *Ernani*. Next was Jacchia's *Hymn to Rossini*, featuring soprano **Grace Hunter** ('46) and baritone **George Constanza** ('50) with the Conservatory Chorus. Finally, Conservatory student **Marvin Finkle** played Gershwin's *Piano Concerto in F*.

Top right: George Brambilla; *Center:* Albert Alphin; *Bottom:* Agide Jacchia

Centennial Concert Series 1867-1967
Boston Conservatory of Music

AUDITORIUM   31 HEMENWAY STREET

SATURDAY AFTERNOON, FEBRUARY 11, 1967*, AT 4:00

CONCERT BY THE CONSERVATORY ORCHESTRA
ROUBEN GREGORIAN, *Conductor*

Programme

I

Festive Overture, Op. 96	*Shostakovitch*
Ritorna Vincitor, from Aïda	*Verdi*
MABLE McKENNEY ('64), *Soprano*	
Ernani, involami, from Ernani	*Verdi*
EVELYN KAZANJIAN ('65), *Soprano*	
Cantata, Hymn to Rossini	*Jacchia*

Words by AUGUSTO FERRERO
English Translation by IRIDE PILLA ('24)

GRACE HUNTER ('46), *Soprano*
GEORGE COSTANZA ('50), *Baritone*

This work is performed in memory of AGIDE JACCHIA,
Director of the Boston Conservatory 1920-1932

II

Concerto in F, for piano and orchestra	*Gershwin*
Allegro	
Andante con moto	
Allegro agitato	

MARVIN FINKLE, *Pianist*

* The Boston Conservatory of Music opened Monday, February 11, 1867, one hundred years ago today. It was the first Conservatory of Music established in the United States.

Seully Hall

Seully Hall, one of the Conservatory's main performance spaces, was previously the site of a Boston Medical Library Association lecture hall. **John Jacob Seully**, for whom the hall is named, was a cantor who lived in the suburbs of Boston. Upon his passing in 1980, an estate gift was used to renovate the hall to its original splendor, including the removal of a drop ceiling, which covered the ornate arches that are a main feature of the space today.

In 2013, the Massachusetts Cultural Council provided a grant for further renovations, most noticeably relocating the stage to the left-hand side of the room to allow for a handicap-accessible backstage area for artists. Seully himself had no clear affiliation with Boston Conservatory, but his gift to "a Boston Conservatory" has benefited students, faculty, and audiences for more than thirty years.

JOHN JACOB SEULLY HALL

DEDICATION CONCERT

Tuesday, March 22, 1988

Fanfare from St. Edmundsbury   Benjamin Britten
Trumpets: Kim Stewart, Robert Stone,
Roy Miller

Opening remarks
William A. Seymour, president
The Boston Conservatory

"The Answer" Op. 21, No. 4   Sergey Rachmaninoff
"Spring Waters" Op. 14, No. 11
Bruce Kolb, tenor

The Pearl Fishers   Georges Bizet
"Au fond du Temple Saint"
Bruce Kolb, tenor
Robert Honeysucker, baritone

Dedication
Mr. Seymour

Quartet in F Major, Op. 59, No. 1   Ludwig van Beethoven

Zoia Bologovsky, violin
Kaede Kobayashi, violin
Leo Mayer, viola
Elizabeth Reardon, cello

Sextour for Piano and Winds   Francis Poulenc
Divertissement
Allegro vivace

Suzanne Kirton, flute   Rick Ward, horn
Yunsun Kim, oboe   Janice Bishop, bassoon
Dawn Aikens, clarinet   Nadya Ilyin, piano

The Modern Era

1967–2015

With the campus formally set in the Fenway neighborhood,

the next era of the school was marked by growth and development that set the stage for the school's present-day structure. During this period of maturation (1967–2015), the Dance, Music, and Theater Divisions settled into a rhythm and found their footing with steady leadership that helped the school earn a reputation for offering the best theater, contemporary dance, and voice/opera training programs in the nation.

Also during this period, the Conservatory expanded its community programming work and, by 2015, was presenting more than 130 performances annually at organizations around Greater Boston, including retirement homes, shelters, veterans organizations, and youth programs.

As the school refined its focus and operations, it experienced a cultural recharge that would quickly distinguish the Conservatory from its peer institutions: the administration, faculty, and staff sought to create a nurturing, student-centric environment that focused on student support and encouragement, rather than rivalry and competition. This philosophy of safe growth and exploration was, until this point, a rarity in performing arts training, as the fields are—by nature—high stakes and high pressure. The Conservatory's more humane approach to training talented young artists quickly became its trademark, fostering an environment in which students felt free to be more experimental and collaborative across disciplines.

During this era, there was an outpouring of multidisciplinary and hybrid work from students and faculty. By the end of the twentieth century, the school was poised at the forefront of performing arts training and creation.

Richard Ortner

Boston Conservatory President **Richard Ortner** transformed the institution with new faculty appointments, construction of state-of-the-art facilities, groundbreaking programs for individuals with special needs, and a merger with Berklee. In October 2016, Ortner announced that he would retire in June 2017, concluding an impressive nineteen-year run as president.

"I've been doing this for a long time, and institutions absolutely require the ability to refresh their leadership periodically," Ortner told *The Boston Globe* in an interview following the announcement of his retirement. "It's been the privilege of a lifetime to have served in this position," he said in another interview. "The next generation of leaders has tremendous opportunity—and I'll look forward to seeing where they take it!"

Ortner is one of Boston's most respected arts leaders, with a forty-year career that began with a summer job with the Boston Symphony Orchestra (BSO) at Tanglewood on a recommendation from **Leonard Bernstein**. Ortner succeeded

William A. Seymour as president of the Conservatory in 1998 and is the eighth person to formally hold this title. Ortner has agreed to remain active with the school after his retirement, taking on a senior advisor role that is focused on enhancing the Conservatory's international reputation, expanding the Board, and developing strategies for the Dance, Music, and Theater Divisions."

"Richard is a living encyclopedia of musical and artistic knowledge," said Berklee President **Roger H. Brown**. "His passion for the Conservatory is palpable, and through his stewardship, he helped create one of the top musical theater programs in the country, the number-one-rated contemporary dance program in the United States, and a classical conservatory that is at once rigorous and humane. The fruits of his vision, particularly the merger of The Boston Conservatory and Berklee, will be harvested for generations to come."

After working at Tanglewood as a guide in 1973, Ortner soon became assistant administrator of the Tanglewood Music

Center, the BSO's renowned academy for advanced training in music. In the years that followed, he developed a thorough overview of major orchestra and festival operations, from concert production and programming to faculty engagement, facilities, fundraising, and board relations.

In 1984, Ortner became administrator of the center, which at the time was under the tripartite artistic leadership of Leonard Bernstein, **Gunther Schuller**, and **Seiji Ozawa**. Ortner helped create Ozawa Hall and Tanglewood's expanded campus. He also helped revive the opera program and contributed to the extraordinary breadth of programming at the annual Festival of Contemporary Music. At Tanglewood, he worked with virtually every major classical artist of the day and two generations of the world's best emerging artists.

His twenty-three-year career with the BSO ended in 1997 amid controversy covered by *The Boston Globe* and *The New York Times*. After a serious difference of opinion regarding the direction of

Boston Conservatory chief spreads his wings

Music

By ELLEN PFEIFER

The last week of May was one of the most mind-bending periods of Richard Ortner's life. He celebrated his 50th birthday, marked the first anniversary of his involuntary departure as administrator of the Tanglewood Music Center, and was appointed president of Boston Conservatory.

It was reminiscent of Richard Strauss' tone poem, "Death and Transfiguration."

The new job will place Ortner at the head of an institution located just a few blocks from Symphony Hall, where he worked with the Boston Symphony Orchestra during the

Tanglewood Music Center, music director Ozawa asked Ortner to resign. According to the *Times*, Ortner was a revered figure at the organization, and faculty and staff were audibly upset upon learning of his termination. Ortner remained at the BSO for another nine months, as the organization sorted through complex management issues that had arisen. It was during this time that he came to the attention of the Conservatory, which was looking for its next president.

"Richard and I were professional friends. We had interacted in BSO affairs, we had a number of friends in common, and I didn't need to read his resume to know whether he fit our needs," said **JoAnne Dickinson**, who led the search as a member and cochair of the Conservatory's Board of Trustees. Effusive about his background, Dickinson added: "He knew the inner workings of institutions, having served

in top positions with the Symphony in Boston and Tanglewood. He had enviable contacts within the musical world; he was no stranger to cultivating donors; he was charming; he had incredible energy; and beyond administrative talents, he was a musician himself, and he knew when the music was good and when it wasn't."

From the start of his presidency in 1998, Ortner drew on his administrative career with the BSO in shaping the Conservatory.

With the needs of his students in mind, he expanded programs and hired exceptional artist-faculty who had unique abilities to guide the progress of his emerging artists. He encouraged the institution to become a leader in the field of special-needs music teacher training, creating unique, cutting-edge programs focused on music and autism. He also secured funds to renovate the Conservatory's historic Hemenway

Street building—updating the mainstage theater and adding four new dance studios—and build a 20,000-square-foot studio building on Ipswich Street just a few years later. The two projects required more than $50 million in fundraising and long-term financing. As of 2016, a second buildable lot remained at the Ipswich Street site for further expansion.

In the latter part of his tenure, Ortner was called a visionary for recognizing how joining with Berklee would add immense value for Conservatory students, creating what he called "the world's most comprehensive and dynamic training ground for global careers in music, dance, theater, and related professions."

His vision was recognized beyond campus. "Richard has always been motivated by his passion for creative expression, and for nurturing young talent," said **Yo-Yo Ma**,

Left: Richard Ortner and cellist/conductor Mstislav Rostropovich at Tanglewood Music Center, circa 1975; *Right*: Marillyn Zacharis and Richard Ortner

the celebrated multiple Grammy Award–winning cellist. "Under his leadership, The Boston Conservatory experienced tremendous artistic growth. He has been indefatigable in reaching out to locate a broad talent pool, and in looking for different ways to think about the performing arts and their role in society. The richness of his contributions is only matched by the richness of his inner cultivation."

The merger of The Boston Conservatory and Berklee—which established Boston Conservatory at Berklee—became official in June 2016 but, in many ways the process began earlier with collaborations around crossregistration, shared faculty, and the founding of the Boston Arts Academy. The vision behind the merger was to create a combined institution that allowed infinite new possibilities for the creation of new music, dance, and theater, reduced the boundaries between

art forms, and dramatically enhanced the ability of graduates to develop and sustain successful careers in the arts.

The merger took several years to develop. "Starting around 2013, we took a hard look at what the Conservatory would need in order to thrive in the coming decades," Ortner said. "The rapidly evolving world of careers for young performers would require students to access new technology resources, greater diversity of repertoire and performance experience, new business and entrepreneurial skills, and a truly global reach. We looked at several potential partners, each of whom could offer a *portion* of what we were looking for—but how extraordinary that we found virtually everything we sought, right next door."

Ortner went on to explain, "For Berklee's part, their strong desire for world-class musical theater and dance resources and

access to conservatory-level ensembles made this a partnership we both wanted to pursue. It was the last thing I felt I needed to accomplish [at the Conservatory]. Done right, the next 150 years will be brilliant!"

Ortner was among the founding Board of Governors of the Boston Arts Academy—Boston's first and only high school for the visual and performing arts, which opened in 1998—and he chaired its Board of Trustees for two years. He has served on the Board of Overseers of the Handel and Haydn Society, the Board of Visitors for Fenway Community Health Center, and the Planning Task Force for Greater Boston's New Center for Arts and Culture. He also served as a panelist for the National Endowment for the Arts and the Aaron Copland Fund for Music, and been an advisor to schools and performing arts institutions throughout the Commonwealth.

Julie Ince Thompson and Her Benediction

Julie Ince Thompson, once called "one of the finest dancers and choreographers to grace the Boston stage" by *The Boston Globe*'s dance critic **Christine Temin**, celebrated many firsts in her career. Among those, she is credited with being one of the first to introduce the Alexander Technique to the Conservatory's curriculum.

Thompson studied theater at the University of California at Santa Barbara, but had no formal dance training. "She embraced dance so quickly and passionately after moving to Cambridge in 1972 that she eventually taught at Harvard Summer Dance Center," Temin wrote. Thompson was a popular collaborator and teacher, but as a dancer she was known for long lines often displayed in solo performances.

Thompson, who taught modern dance and, as the course catalog listed it, "proprioceptive movement technique," was on the Conservatory's faculty when she died on September 25, 2003 from complications due to colon cancer. She was one day shy of her fifty-second birthday.

"Her life and art shimmered on the edge between this and other worlds," composer **Patricia Van Ness**, a frequent collaborator of Thompson's, told *The Boston Globe* for Thompson's obituary.

Thompson's husband, **Tommy**, and daughter, **Danielle**, established a dance scholarship in her memory at the Conservatory, the Julie Ince Thompson Award Scholarship.

Thompson's voice lives on as the author of the Conservatory's commencement invocation and benediction,* which is still used more than ten years after her passing:

The Julie Ince Thompson Benediction

May the blessing and grace of this day
inspirit you
with
joy
fierce passion
perseverance
and
courage
go now
from the blessing of this day
to
stake the claim of your lives
on the
farthest reach of
your dreams
with conviction
with dedication
with assurance
go now
from the ceremony of this day
to do
what you have been called to do
because
you
can
because
you
are able
because
you
must
Go now
with tenderness and love
to
make of yourselves
a
light
in our imperfect and oh so beautiful
world
Shine brightly!
                              —*Julie Ince Thompson*

Bottom: Tommy Neblett, dance faculty, Tommy Thompson, Key'Aira Lockett, scholarship student, and Danielle Thompson

 # ProArts Consortium

Boston Conservatory and Berklee College of Music are two of the six founding organizations of the **Professional Arts (ProArts) Consortium**, an association of Boston institutions of higher education dedicated to the visual and performing arts.

The consortium was incorporated in 1984 and, at the time, included Boston Conservatory, Berklee College of Music, Boston Architectural College, Emerson College, the Massachusetts College of Art and Design, and the School of the Museum of Fine Arts. It was later joined by New England Conservatory of Music.

As founding members of the ProArts Consortium, the Conservatory and Berklee played key roles in establishing the **Boston Arts Academy**, the city's first public high school for the visual and performing arts, located across from Fenway Park. That effort was supported by then **Mayor Thomas M. Menino**, who complimented how the high school had become "a beacon for many students who found the guidance to develop as artists."

Conservatory Staff and the Creation of a Culture

There are many reasons that prospective students choose to attend Boston Conservatory, but the biggest draw, students say, is the small but dedicated faculty and staff who work tirelessly to make their college experience extraordinary. In many cases, the Conservatory's staff and leadership are the ones who students have the most contact with over their time at the school. The staff profiled here are just a handful of the remarkable individuals whose devotion and compassion have helped shaped the Conservatory's culture.

When **Yousef Hezar Djeribian**, chef and owner of the bustling Counterpoint Café, died in February 2015, the Conservatory didn't just lose an employee; it lost an integral part of the community. Alumni, faculty, and students recounted how Djeribian made students feel welcome at the café and always took care of them—from giving out meals when students were low on cash to attending hundreds of performances. Upon his passing, Djeribian's family asked that, in lieu of flowers, donations be made to the school in his name to commemorate his love.

It would be hard to find anyone who has had a greater impact on Conservatory student life than **Carmen S. Griggs**, former dean of students. Many, including President **Richard Ortner** and his predecessor **William A. Seymour**, credit Griggs with being a leader in creating the caring and nurturing student-centric culture for which the Conservatory is so well known. Evidence of Griggs's legacy can be found in every corner of the campus. After joining the Conservatory in 1988, Griggs, a former social worker and English teacher, organized the school's first-ever student affairs team, launched the school's first-ever health and wellness programs, established a formal structure for residence halls and life outside the classroom, and created numerous handbooks and resource materials to help students and staff navigate modern city life. Safety and wellbeing were at the core of Griggs's efforts. Alumni often recount seeing her at performances to support students or checking in after hours to make sure everything was okay. Whereas many performing arts schools are noted to be competitive and "cut-throat," the Conservatory is recognized for having a supportive and nurturing

environment—thanks to the tireless work of staff members like Griggs.

James Bynum was an administrative assistant whose title belied the many roles he played and the behind-the-scenes work he did in his thirty-eight years at the Conservatory. For many alumni, his caring nature made the Conservatory feel like home. Some of his most memorable accomplishments include organizing trips for students in the Dance Division to perform in Europe, and, through his work in the financial aid office, helping find opportunities for students to work or gain scholarships.

Once he joined The Boston Conservatory, he was hooked. **Richard Malcolm** (B.M. '77, percussion), an alumnus who immediately began work in the school's audio/visual (AV) office after graduating, has been with the Conservatory for thirty-eight years and counting. The longest-serving staff member in recent history, Malcolm has always shown a dedication and support that is appreciated by the countless performers, faculty, and staff whom he helped in his role as director of AV. From filming thousands of recitals and performances to

Carmen S. Griggs

Lawrence Isaacson

Kim Haack with student Matt Lowy (B.M. '15, composition)

preparing countless resources for classroom instruction, Malcolm always finds a way for "the show to go on."

Standing at 6'9," **James (Jim) O'Dell**, current associate dean for academic operations and former music division director, has a towering physical presence that is dwarfed only by his dedication to the Conservatory and its students. O'Dell has been a fixture at the school since 1988. At the time, there was a 6'5" master's student pianist—**Mike Bartell**—who would later become the Conservatory's very first information technology (IT) director and lead the first campus-wide installation of computers. Impressed by how O'Dell's height surpassed his own, Bartell nicknamed him "Chief" in reference to the 6'10" **Kevin McHale** of the Boston Celtics. Over the years, O'Dell would assume many roles, including chair, director, assistant and associate dean of academic affairs, interim dean of the Conservatory, and interim vice president for academic affairs and dean of the Conservatory.

Lawrence (Larry) Isaacson has been a steady force in the Music Division, first in 1985 as a studio instructor teaching trombone and conductor of The Boston Conservatory Wind Ensemble, and then shifting as an administrator some fifteen years into his tenure. As the associate director of the Music Division, Isaacson has worked with three Music Division directors to keep the school's music programs current on new technologies and platforms. He also oversees the Conservatory's robust ensemble programs, which is a core component of the Music Division's training. Outside the classroom, Isaacson stays involved in Boston's music scene through his work as music director and conductor for Symphony Nova, a Boston-based nonprofit that he founded in 2007 for music school graduates to gain performance experience and develop professionally.

Kim Haack's generosity and kindness make her an unforgettable part of The Boston Conservatory for all who meet her. Though her title on paper is

Director of External Relations and her community relations work is extensive, Haack does much more for students and staff alike. In addition to serving as a liaison between the Conservatory and the city of Boston, Haack also oversees the school's robust community outreach program, Conservatory Connections. Founded in 1999, the program organizes student performance groups and presents more than 130 performances each year to forty-plus community partners, such as retirement homes and shelters. Under Haack's leadership, the program garners 38-percent student participation annually. Haack is also credited by many students and alumni as being a devoted mentor, and for providing important encouragement and support during challenging times. A testament to the respect she has garnered over the years, Conservatory colleagues nominated her to be the school's merger liaison to oversee operations during the first few years of the merger with Berklee.

115

Conservatory Connections

For 150 years, Boston Conservatory has shared its resources and talent with the community at large, earning a reputation early on for being vital to the culture and growth of the city. Today, that work is embodied not only in the range of free and low-cost performances offered each year, but also through the mission of Conservatory Connections.

Conservatory Connections is a robust community outreach program that brings the arts to audiences who are unable to travel to campus to attend traditional performances. In a given year, Conservatory Connections presents more than 130 performances to 40-plus community partners that include shelters, assisted living facilities, community centers, and veterans organizations. It also offers a number of community engagement programs, such as dance classes for children on the autism spectrum and movement classes for low-mobility senior citizens.

Founded in 1999, Conservatory Connections is all-inclusive and has 38-percent student participation each year. As of 2016, it consists of performance outreach, community classes, and autism-related programming. Ensemble groups, including the Troubadors (opera), Cabaret (theater), and Chamber Music, perform for community partners citywide, while Autism-Friendly Performances invite special needs children and families on campus to experience live theater in a thoughtfully designed environment. Additionally, many partnering organizations receive free tickets to shows and concerts at the Conservatory throughout the year.

"Each program or performance is tailored to the location and the audience," said director of external relations **Kim Haack**, who oversees the Conservatory Connections Program. "We hope to cultivate programming around our new contemporary theater program in the future," she added. "Performing in an unconventional space such as a museum adds life and sound to visual art that enhances the experience. We often use the collection as inspiration for our concert content; it allows our students a chance to explore and recognize the commonalities of all artists."

In January 2016, patrons of the Museum of Fine Arts in Boston enjoyed John Cage's *Song Books*, inspired by the I-Ching, and performed throughout the Chinese Galleries by six Conservatory voice students: **Rachel Barg** (B.M. '16), **Lauren Cook** (M.M. '16), **Simon Dyer** (G.P.D. '17), **Natalie Logan** (M.M. '16), **Andrew O'Shanick** (M.M. '16), and **Tzytle Steinman** (B.M. '16). Dyer organized and produced the performance, which was coached by the school's 2015–2016 Kunkemueller Artist in Residence, famed soprano **Tony Arnold.**

The Conservatory Connections program was founded by a group of students who did not want to lose sight of why they were training for a life in the arts: to tell stories, to inspire dialogues, and to connect with others. These students had a vision of bringing the arts to underserved audiences and made it their mission to use performance as a way of empowering others to live fuller, healthier lives.

In the 2015–2016 academic year, funding for the Conservatory Connections program came through grants from The Hamilton Company Charitable Foundation, the Seth Sprague Educational and Charitable Foundation, the Adelard A. Roy and Valeda Lea Roy Foundation, and the Boston Cultural Council, a local agency supported by the Massachusetts Cultural Council, a state agency.

2015–2016 Conservatory Connections partners include: Boston Public Library; Boston Public Market; Boston Children's Museum; The Boston Home; Cafe Emmanuel/ETHOS Lunch Group, a program for gay and lesbian elders from Fenway Health; Center Communities of Brookline; Dana-Farber Cancer Institute; Fenway Studios; Franklin Square House; Hale House; The Hurley School; Landmark at Longwood; Massachusetts General Hospital Cancer Center; Massachusetts General Hospital's Senior HealthWISE Program; Michael Driscoll School; Morville House; Museum of Fine Arts, Boston; Rogerson House's Alzheimer's Day Care Program; Rosie's Place; Susan Bailis Assisted Living; Symphony Park, Fenway; United South End Settlements; and YMCA.

Judson Evans and The Garden

Boston Conservatory Liberal Arts Division Director **Judson Evans** believes that teaching performing artists the art of language will help them better express themselves through performance. One example of this on campus is The Garden, a student-run poetry group that has published an annual collection of original poems since 1996.

Evans, who has served as the group's advisor since it was founded, describes the student group as "a place for students with special interests in poetry, prose, and creative writing from all divisions and all backgrounds." Evans has been on the Conservatory's faculty since 1984, teaching courses in literature, expression, and communication.

For some students, the group inspires new career paths. **Eric Hollander** (B.M. '14) was a viola performance major and former editor of the eponymous publication. "*The Garden* gave me a platform to express my interests in literature and poetry

on my own terms," he said. His work with the group encouraged him to pursue a graduate degree in writing and publishing at Depauw University in Chicago, where he also founded a musical group dedicated to "creating a tangible process of literary interpretation through music."

In 2016, The Garden published its twentieth annual volume. Each volume has a creative theme that challenges the poets and their audience to explore the worlds of poetry and self-expression through a unique lens. Themes have included "Graffiti," "Mood Swing," and "Linked Verse."

The group meets regularly throughout the academic year to host workshops and review poems that have been submitted for consideration. The months-long process of publishing *The Garden* culminates in an annual, open-invitation publication party, which is held each April. Here, the poets read their work aloud and celebrate their literary accomplishment with friends.

"Students remember their experience with *The Garden* long after they have moved on from the Conservatory," Evans said. "Perhaps they remember *The Garden* because it provides them the chance to leave a mark, in print, within the Conservatory's walls."

An award-winning poet, Evans practices the same collaborative approach in his own creative work. He has partnered with actors, dancers, and musicians in the Boston area for a variety of projects, including the poetic monologue *Scrabble Ridge,* which was performed by the late choreographer and performance artist **Julie Ince Thompson** as part of the Fleet Boston Celebrity Series in January 2001. He also cocreated the musical monodrama *Wintering the Queen*, a collaboration with composer, teacher, and Conservatory alumnus **Rudolf Rojahn** (M.M. '04, composition).

Lynn Chang

Lynn Chang's artistry on the violin is evident from his illustrious career as a performer, but his influence extends beyond concert halls through the many successes of his students.

Chang has been on the violin faculty of Boston Conservatory since 1983. He also teaches at New England Conservatory of Music and Boston University, instructs students privately at his alma mater, Harvard University, and is an affiliated artist at the Massachusetts Institute of Technology (MIT). A founding member

of the Boston Chamber Music Society, he directs the Conservatory's honors ensemble, the Hemenway Strings.

Some of the many students that Chang has taught include **Ala Jojatu** (G.P.D. '02, violin) of the Boston Symphony Orchestra, **Joseph Lin**, first violinist of the Juilliard String Quartet, and **Johnny Lee** and **Akiko Terumoto** of the Los Angeles Philharmonic.

Chang has also collaborated with **Yo-Yo Ma**, including his Silk Road Project and its 2004 residency at the Peabody Essex

Museum. In 2011, when the Kennedy Center Honors recognized Ma, Chang was invited to perform for the ceremony along with musicians **Pamela Frank**, **Sharon Robinson**, **Jaime Laredo**, and **Emmanuel Ax**.

Among his many personal achievements, Chang was the top prizewinner at the International Paganini Competition in Genoa, Italy, and was a soloist at the 2010 Nobel Peace Prize ceremony in Oslo, Norway, which honored Peace Prize laureate **Liu Xiaobo**.

Neil Donohoe

Almost every student who has auditioned for a spot in the Boston Conservatory's musical theater program in the last thirty years is likely to have seen the same person during his or her audition: Dean of Theater **Neil Donohoe**. The dean sits in on every audition, a rarity that does not go unnoticed as evidence of his commitment to his department.

Donohoe, who has been head of the Theater Division since 1985, has sparked innovation at the Conservatory in a number of areas and has overseen tremendous growth in the division, which has made it one of the leading musical theater programs in the world. He pioneered what is now considered a standard for performing arts schools—an annual showcase performance in New York City in which senior musical theater students present a program of musical numbers

to industry professionals. In keeping with the times, Donohoe also introduced an online version of the event in 2016, calling it a "webcase," or online collection of portfolio videos designed to give students more industry exposure in New York City and beyond.

An active director and producer, Donohoe has led productions both at the Conservatory and in Boston's rich performance community. He also coproduced the Conservatory's 125th anniversary celebration, which featured a concert starring **Marvin Hamlisch** and **Liz Callaway**, and he has been a producer of the Kurt Weill Festival.

Donohoe's directing credits at the Conservatory include several world and local premieres (*The Human Comedy*, *Angels*, *The Screams of Kitty Genovese*)

and adaptations of classic shows (*Candide*, *West Side Story*). He also codirected, adapted, and produced a full production of *Die Fledermaus*, which ran at the Emerson Cutler Majestic Theater in 1997 to positive reviews.

Donohoe's off-campus credits include producing a benefit production of *Elegies for Angels, Punks and Raging Queens* (a Boston premiere) for Boston Living Center, and a benefit for the Fenway Community Health Center starring **Madeline Kahn**. He served as director of the annual Vincent Show for ten years, which raised money for the Women's Care Division of Massachusetts General Hospital, and coordinated performers for the Boston Pops Fourth of July Fireworks Spectacular from 1998 to 2001.

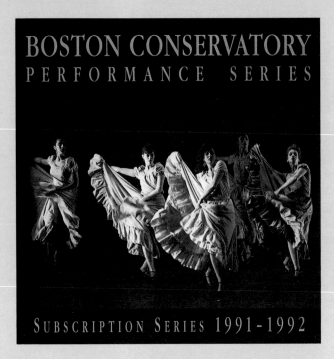

BOSTON CONSERVATORY
PERFORMANCE SERIES

SUBSCRIPTION SERIES 1991-1992

the **Boston Conservatory**

125th Anniversary

GALA PERFORMANCE

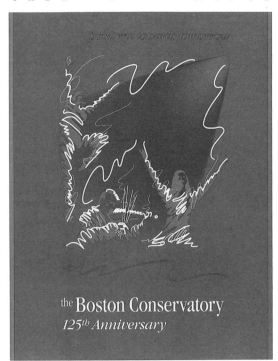

point me towards tomorrow

the **Boston Conservatory**
125th Anniversary

AT SYMPHONY HALL

point me towards tomorrow

Letter from the President

Dear Friends,

As most of you know, this year marks the 125th Anniversary of The Boston Conservatory. In February of 1867, an upstairs studio at 154 Boylston Street was the origin of an extended and fruitful history of training in the performing arts. That our institution today continues to be a significant force in the preparation of young artists is a tribute to the thousands of students, teachers, administrators and alumni that have passed through its doors. Just as these passing years have seen enormous change and development in our country and in society in general, the performing arts also have changed and expanded. The Boston Conservatory has consistently stayed abreast of development in the arts and is today an internationally recognized school of the performing arts.

With a student body representative of nearly every state in our country and more than twenty-five foreign countries, and a faculty of celebrated performing artists and recognized pedagogues, The Boston Conservatory has rightfully taken its place as a leading arts institution.

It is vital that we remember, however, that a successful past is best considered as the foundation upon which to build a positive and fruitful future. We purposely adopted as our anniversary motto the phrase, "Point me towards tomorrow," in order that we might visibly express our determination to remain a relevant, innovative, inventive arts-training institution in the coming years.

Looking back at our 125-year history with pride, we look forward to the future with hope. Here's to another 125 years!

Cordially,

William A. Seymour
President
The Boston Conservatory

the Boston Conservatory   *125th Anniversary*
8 The Fenway Boston, Massachusetts 02215   (617) 536-6340   FAX (617) 536-3176

THE BOSTON CONSERVATORY 125TH ANNIVERSARY FESTIVAL

presents

a benefit performance addressing the crisis of arts education for the future

Point Me Towards Tomorrow
an artist's journey

inspired by monologues created by students of Hope High School, Providence, Rhode Island

Starring

Liz Callaway	**Angelina Réaux**	**Robert Honeysucker**
Maureen Brennan	**Stephen Lehew**	**Larry Watson**
Jacqulyn Buglisi	**Peter DiMuro**	**Derek Smith**
Terrence Yancey	**Matthew Lashey**	**Megan Johnson**
	David Benoit	

and ensembles from
The Boston Conservatory, Youth pro Musica, and Needham High School

With Special Guest Star
Marvin Hamlisch

Featuring music created or selected for this event by composers

David Shire	**Galt MacDermot**	**Henry Krieger**
Marvin Hamlisch	**Charles Strouse**	**John Morris**
	Ricky Ian Gordon	

Additional music performed with kind permission from composers

Stephen Sondheim   **Janet Hood**

Conceived and Directed by
Neil Donohoe

Music Produced, Coordinated and Directed by
Cathy Rand

Conducted by
Ronald Feldman

Associate Producer
Troy Siegfreid

Producers
Allison Ball & Neil Donohoe

---

the Boston Conservatory

Presents

*The 125th Anniversary
Performance Festival*

February 7 – March 8, 1992

125th Anniversary

In 1992, **Neil Donohoe** and **Allison Ball** produced "Point Me Towards Tomorrow," a celebration of the Conservatory's 125th anniversary, which included a series of workshops, lectures, and a festival addressing the crisis of arts education for the future. The cast featured many notable faculty, such as **Robert Honeysucker** and **Maureen Brennan**, with special guest star **Marvin Hamlisch**. The gala itself honored Conservatory "greats" **Ruth Sandholm Ambrose** (dance), **Iride Pilla** (voice/opera), **H. Wilfred Churchill** (music), **Attilio Poto** (music), and **Robert Leibacher** (theater).

A New M.F.A. Degree in Musical Theater

In 2012, The Boston Conservatory became the first school of its kind and only the second college in the country to offer a master of fine arts degree in musical theater, the terminal degree for this field of study.

Nationally known for its musical theater training program and large number of alumni working on Broadway, the Conservatory previously only offered a bachelor of fine arts in musical theater at the undergraduate level, and—until 2012—a master of music in musical theater at the graduate level.

"We have a track record of preparing and graduating students who consistently get work on Broadway, in national tours, and in television and film," says **Neil Donohoe**, dean of theater at the Conservatory. "Given the strength and reputation of our program, it made sense for us to further expand our leadership in this area and offer the terminal degree for older students seeking careers in theater."

The Massachusetts Department of Education approved the Conservatory's proposal on February 28, 2012, following an extensive, seven-month preparation and review period. The sixty-credit-hour M.F.A. degree requires five semesters of study, including one intensive summer session, which allows students to complete the program in just two years—a distinction from those M.F.A. programs requiring three years of study. The Conservatory's program enrolled its inaugural class in September 2012.

The Big Break

Morgan Hernandez, Mackenzie Lesser-Roy, and MiMi Scardulla

The "big break" can happen at any time; one just has to be ready when the opportunity comes. In 2015, three students at The Boston Conservatory were ready and soon found themselves performing on some of the nation's biggest stages.

Morgan Hernandez (B.F.A. '19, musical theater) had just started her freshman year at the Conservatory and was still finding her way around campus when she was selected to play Maria in *West Side Story* opposite Skylar Astin (*Spring Awakening, Pitch Perfect*) in the 2016 limited-run production, which was presented by Carnegie Hall's Weill Music Institute.

Mackenzie Lesser-Roy (B.F.A. '17, musical theater) was a junior studying musical theater when she landed the lead role of Girl in *Once* for the 2016 national tour of the Tony Award–winning musical, based on the Academy Award–winning film of the same name. Lesser-Roy, an accomplished cellist and pianist, starred as the young Czech musician who captures the heart of an Irish busker in the show, which had a twenty-seven-city tour. Reflecting on her training, Lesser-Roy explained, "My Conservatory education not only taught me how to create a character on stage, but also how to maintain that character over a period of time and act as a professional in the real world."

MiMi Scardulla (associate alumna '16, musical theater) was in her senior year at the Conservatory when she made her Off-Broadway debut as Lydia in *Gigantic*, a new musical about a teen weight-loss camp, which played at the Acorn Theater in New York in 2015. Scardulla described her character as a "kooky Goth camper who loves to dance."

Top row: Morgan Hernandez rehearsing with Skylar Astin for *West Side Story,* 2016;
Middle row: Mackenzie Lesser-Roy and Sam Cieri in the national tour of *Once,* 2016;
Bottom row: MiMi Scardulla and Zachary Jones in the Conservatory's production of *On the Town,* 2015

Alumni Working in Theater, Film, and Television

The Boston Conservatory Theater Division has fostered numerous successful performers who have gone on to receive accolades in their field. The list below is only a fraction of those who have been formally recognized. *Note: The Conservatory defines an associate alumni as anyone who attended the Conservatory for at least two consecutive semesters and left on good academic standing.*

Nick Adams, B.F.A. '05, musical theater. Broadway: *Priscilla Queen of the Desert*, *Chicago*, and *Guys and Dolls*

Gerard Alessandrini, B.F.A. '77, musical theater. Broadway: Creator, *Forbidden Broadway*

David Benoit, G.P.D. '88, musical theater. Broadway: *Jekyll and Hyde*, *Avenue Q*, *Les Misérables*, and *Dance of the Vampire*

Adam Berry, B.F.A. '05, musical theater. Television: *Point Society*, *Paranormal Lockdown*, and *Ghost Hunters*

Jay Binder, associate alumnus '70, theater. Broadway: More than seventy credits for casting, producing, and design since 1980, including *Jerome Robbins'*

Broadway, *Lost in Yonkers*, *Chicago*, *The Lion King*, *Urinetown*, *Movin' Out*, *Lestat*, *The 39 Steps*, *Nice Work If You Can Get It*, and *A Gentlemen's Guide to Love & Murder*; Television: *I'll Fly Away* and *The Music Man*, casting; Film: *Chicago*, *Hairspray*, and *Nine*, casting

Allison Blackwell, M.M. '04, musical theater. Broadway: *The Gershwins' Porgy and Bess* and *One Night with Janis Joplin*

Will Blum, B.F.A. '07, musical theater. Broadway: *The Book of Mormon*, *School of Rock—The Musical*, and *Grease*

Erick Buckley, B.F.A. '89, musical theater. Broadway: *The Addams Family*, *Motown: The Musical*, and *The Phantom of the Opera*

Gabrielle Carrubba, B.F.A. '18, musical theater. Television: *The Avatars* and *American Idol: Season 11*

Stephen Cerf, associate alumnus '10, musical theater. Broadway: *Motown: The Musical* and *Jersey Boys*

Angela Christian, B.F.A. '92, musical theater. Broadway: *The Woman in White*,

Thoroughly Modern Millie, and *James Joyce's The Dead*

Nicholas Christopher, associate alumnus '12, musical theater. Broadway: *Motown: The Musical*, *Hamilton*, and *Miss Saigon*

Adam Dannheisser, B.F.A. '92, musical theater. Broadway: *Rock of Ages*

Erin Davie, B.F.A. '00, musical theater. Broadway: *A Little Night Music*, *Side Show*, *The Mystery of Edwin Drood*, *Curtains*, and *Grey Gardens*; Television: *Orange Is the New Black* and *The Good Wife*; Film: *King Jack* and *Easter Mysteries*

Laura Marie Duncan, B.F.A. '94, musical theater. Broadway: *Billy Elliot: The Musical*, *Dirty Rotten Scoundrels*, *South Pacific*, and *The Full Monty*

Andrew Durand, B.F.A. '08, musical theater. Broadway: *Spring Awakening* and *War Horse*; Television: *Madam Secretary*

Laura Dreyfuss, B.F.A. '10, musical theater. Broadway: *Dear Evan Hansen*, *Once*, and *Hair*; Television: *Glee*

Emily Ferranti, B.F.A. '09, musical theater. Broadway: *Wicked*

Nick Adams

Laura Dreyfuss

Josh Grisetti

Lisa Finegold, B.F.A. '11, musical theater. Broadway: *Rock of Ages*; Film: *Life of An Actress: The Musical* and *Tokyo Heights*

Kimiko Glenn, associate alumna '11, musical theater. Broadway: *Waitress*; Television: *Orange Is the New Black*

Alexandra Frohlinger, B.F.A. '10, musical theater. Broadway: *Soul Doctor*; Television: *Frank and Ernie*

Ben Gettinger, B.F.A. '04, musical theater. Broadway: *Mamma Mia!*; Television: *The Hub*; Film: *Dribbles*

Bradley Gibson, B.F.A. '13, musical theater. Broadway: *Rocky* and *A Bronx Tale*

Susan Goforth, B.F.A. '91, musical theater. Film: *10 Days in a Madhouse*, producer/actor, and *The War of the Worlds*, writer/producer/actor

Josh Grisetti, B.F.A. '04, musical theater. Broadway: *It Shoulda Been You* and

Something Rotten!; Television: *The Knights of Prosperity*; Film: *The Immigrant, Revolutionary Road*, and *The Namesake*

Josie de Guzman, Broadway: *Guys and Dolls, Nick & Nora, West Side Story, Carmelina*, and *Runaways*

Marcy Harriel, B.F.A. '94, musical theater. Broadway: *In the Heights, Lennon*, and *Rent*; Television: *Elementary, Nurse Jackie*, and *Royal Pains*; Film: *Grindhouse*

Kendal Hartse, B.F.A. '07, musical theater. Broadway: *Rodgers & Hammerstein's Cinderella* and *On a Clear Day You Can See Forever*

Luke Hawkins, associate alumnus '07, musical theater. Film: *Hail, Caesar!*, dancer

Mike Heslin, B.F.A. '11, musical theater. Broadway: *War Horse*; Television: *I Love You … But I Lied*; Film: *I Dream Too Much*

Austin Hu, Television: *The Affair* and *Younger*; Film: Nearly a dozen credits, including *Sleeping with Other People*

Colin Israel, B.F.A. '05, musical theater. Broadway: *Matilda: The Musical*

Amy Jo Jackson, B.F.A. '05, musical theater. Broadway: *Mystery of Edwin Drood*, dialect coach

Jason Jurman, B.F.A. '02, musical theater. Broadway: More than a dozen film and television credits, including *Cougar Club, Law & Order: Special Victims Unit*, and *Blue Bloods*

Chad Kimball, B.F.A. '99, musical theater. Broadway: *Memphis* (Tony Award nominee), *Life with Albertine*, and *Lennon*

Jesse Kissel, B.F.A. '06, musical theater. Broadway: *The Visit*, musical director/conductor

Eddie Korbich, B.F.A. '83, musical theater. Broadway: *A Gentleman's Guide to Love & Murder*, *After the Night and the Music*, *Sweeney Todd*, *Carousel*, *Seussical*, *Wicked*, *The Little Mermaid*, *A Christmas Story: The Musical*, and *Breakfast at Tiffany's*

Veronica J. Kuehn, Broadway: *Mamma Mia!*; Television: *Casting*

Nikka Graff Lanzarone, B.F.A. '05, musical theater. Broadway: *Chicago* and *Women on the Verge of a Nervous Breakdown*

Jamie LaVerdiere, B.F.A. '96, musical theater. Broadway: *Motown: The Musical*, *The Pirate Queen*, and *The Producers*

Cedric Leiba, Jr., M.M. '05, musical theater. Film: *Millie and the Lords*

Austin Lesch, B.F.A. '04, musical theater. Broadway: *Something Rotten!*, *Billy Elliot: The Musical*, and *Violet*

Joe Machota, M.M. '95, musical theater. Broadway: *Mamma Mia!*; Casting: Creative Artists Agency (CAA) Theater Department

Rachael MacFarlane, associate alumna, '98, musical theater. Television: Thirty credits as a voice actor for shows including *American Dad!* and *Family Guy*; Film: Three films, including *Ted 2*

Constantine Maroulis, B.F.A. '02, musical theater. Broadway: Tony Award nominee, *Rock of Ages*, *The Wedding Singer*, and *Jekyll and Hyde*, and as a producer, *Spring Awakening* (revival)

Alex Matteo, B.F.A. '11, musical theater. Broadway: *Annie*

Liz McCartney, G.P.D. '88, musical theater. Broadway: *Annie*, *South Pacific*, *Taboo*, *Dance of the Vampires*, *Mamma Mia!*, *Thoroughly Modern Millie*, *Les Misérables*, and *The Phantom of the Opera*

Michael McGrath, associate alumnus '76, musical theater. Broadway: *Nice Work If You Can Get It* (Tony Award winner) *Spamalot* (Tony Award nominee), *My Favorite Year*, *She Loves Me*, *The Goodbye Girl*, *On the Twentieth Century*, *Born Yesterday*, *Memphis*, *Is He Dead?*, *Wonderful Town*, *Little Me*, and *Swinging on a Star*

Katharine McPhee, associate alumna, musical theater. Television: *Scorpion*, *Smash*, and several others; Film: Six film credits, including *Peace, Love & Misunderstanding*

Dan Micciche, B.F.A. '07, musical theater. Broadway: *Chicago*; Television: *Home & Family*

Karen Murphy, B.F.A. '77, musical theater. Broadway: *A Little Night Music*, *9 to 5*, *The Visit*, and *42nd Street*

Anne L. Nathan, B.F.A. '85, musical theater. Broadway: *Once*, *It Shoulda Been You*, *Sunday in the Park with George*, *Ragtime*, *Chicago*, *Assassins*, and *Thoroughly Modern Millie*

Shoba Narayan, B.F.A. '12, musical theater. Television: *Quantico* and *Gossip Girl*; Film: *Growing Up Smith* and *Coin Heist*

Brian Nash, B.M. '00, voice. Broadway: *Camelot*, *Kinky Boots*, and *Brigadoon*, benefit concert

Johnny Newcomb, B.F.A. '11, musical theater. Broadway: *The Last Ship* and *Into the Woods*

Ana Nogueira, B.F.A. '07, musical theater. Television: *The Vampire Diaries*, *The Battery's Down*, *The Michael J. Fox Show*, and others; Film: *You Were Never Here*

Dominic Nolfi, B.F.A. '00, musical theater. Broadway: *Jersey Boys* and *Motown: The Musical*

Jack Noseworthy, B.F.A. '87, dance. Broadway: *Sweet Smell of Success*, *A Chorus Line*, and *Jerome Robbins' Broadway*; Film: More than twenty-five credits, including *Encino Man*, *Surrogates*, *U-571*, and *Julia*

Amos Oliver III, B.F.A. '14, dance. Television: *Hairspray Live*

Weston Wills Olson, M.M. '07, musical theater. Broadway: *Les Misérables*

Emily Pynenburg, B.F.A. '14, musical theater. Broadway: *Gigi* and *Cats*

Noah Racey, B.F.A. '93, musical theater. Broadway: Performer/choreographer: *Curtains*, *Never Gonna Dance*, *Thoroughly Modern Millie*, and *Follies*; Television: *Person of Interest*, *Boardwalk Empire*

Peter Reckell, B.F.A '78, musical theater. Television: More than 1,300 episodes of *Days of Our Lives*

Reva Rice, B.F.A. '83, dance. Broadway: *Fosse*, *Chicago*, and *Starlight Express*

Janet Saia, B.F.A. '90, musical theater. Broadway: *The Phantom of the Opera*

Derek St. Pierre, B.F.A. '10, musical theater. Broadway: *Rock of Ages*

Adam Sanford, B.F.A. '04, musical theater. Broadway: *Wicked*

Drew Sarich, B.F.A. '97, musical theater. Broadway: *Les Misérables* and *Lestat*

Marcy Harriel

Constantine Maroulis

Alysha Umphress

Jack Scott, associate alumnus '14, musical theater. Broadway: *Newsies: The Musical*

Keesha Sharp, B.F.A. '96, musical theater. Television: Two dozen credits including *Girlfriends*, *American Crime Story*, and *Lethal Weapon*; Film: A dozen films, including *Why Did I Get Married?*

Traci Skoldberg, B.F.A. '06, musical theater. Broadway: *Mamma Mia!*; Film: *Containment*

Jason Michael Snow, B.F.A. '06, musical theater. Broadway: *The Book of Mormon* and *South Pacific*

Adam Souza, B.F.A. '04, musical theater. Broadway: *Wicked*, associate musical supervisor

Chelsea Morgan Stock, B.F.A. '07, musical theater. Broadway: *Something Rotten!*, *Sister Act*, and *Baby It's You*

Ilana Ransom Toeplitz, associate alumna '08, musical theater. Broadway: *Violet*

and *A Christmas Story: The Musical*, assistant director

Natalie Toro, B.F.A. '86, musical theater. Television: *Child of the '70s*, *Person of Interest*, and *Elementary*

Santina Umbach, B.F.A. '86, musical theater. Broadway: *Mamma Mia!*

Stephanie Umoh, B.F.A. '08, musical theater. Broadway: *Ragtime*; Television: *NYC 22*; Film: *Big Words*

Alysha Umphress, B.F.A. '04, musical theater. Broadway: *American Idiot* and *On the Town*

Adina Verson, B.F.A. '05, musical theater. Television: *The Strain*

Matt Wall, B.F.A. '95, musical theater. *Something Rotten!*, *Follies*, *Evita*, *Annie*, *How to Succeed in Business Without Really Trying*, *Promises, Promises*, *South Pacific*, *110 in the Shade*, *Curtains*, *The Drowsy Chaperone*, *Dirty Rotten*

Scoundrels, *Thoroughly Modern Millie*, and *Saturday Night Fever*

Thommie Walsh, B.F.A. '72, musical theater. Broadway: Two-time Tony Award winner for choreography, and *A Chorus Line*, *My One and Only*, *Nine*, and *My Favorite Year*

Matt Walton, B.F.A. '95, musical theater. More than fifty film and television credits, including *Burn After Reading*, *The Good Wife*, and *Devious Maids*

Bud Weber, B.F.A. '09, musical theater. Broadway: *Something Rotten!*, *Aladdin*, and *Wicked*

Dan'yelle Williamson, B.F.A. '06, musical theater. Broadway: *Memphis*, *Rocky*, and *Scandalous*

Victor Wisehart, B.F.A. '06, dance. Broadway: *An American in Paris*

Rance Wright, M.M. '06, musical theater. Television: *Four Weddings*

Yasuko "Yasi" Tokunaga

Her twenty–one years as director of the Dance Division were during turbulent and uncertain times for The Boston Conservatory, but **Yasuko "Yasi" Tokunaga** led her department with trademark steely grace.

Tokunaga, called "Yasi" by colleagues and students, was the third person to run the dance program. She took the reins in 1989 from **Ruth Sandholm Ambrose**, who was brought on board by division founder **Jan Veen**. Tokunaga first taught at the Conservatory's summer program in 1972 and was already in residence when she took leadership of the department. Tokunaga came to the Conservatory as a preeminent presenter of works by **Martha Graham**, **José Limón**, and **Paul Taylor**, strengthening the Conservatory's one-of-a-kind degree training that combined modern dance and ballet.

During Tokunaga's early years at the Conservatory, President **William A. Seymour** was beginning to straighten out the school's finances and revamp programs and scholarships to attract the best students. "These were not easy times," said Seymour. "With dance, I always knew we'd be okay with the program because Yasi was there keeping things on track and creating remarkable work."

Under Tokunaga's leadership, the Conservatory secured its first-ever grant for dance from the National Endowment of the Arts to perform a tribute to famed choreographer **Murray Louis**. She also helped the Conservatory become first college to be granted rights to perform four original works created by Martha Graham and José Limón, two works by **Anna Sokolow** and **Alwin Nikolais**, and one work by **Antony Tudor**—an honor for the school and student dancers involved. The Conservatory's performance of Graham's *Appalachian Spring* was so astounding that a video recording of it now sits in the Library of Congress.

Tokunaga retired from the Conservatory in 2011 and launched the Tokunaga Dance Ko. with her sister, Emiko (who also worked at the Conservatory) in New York City. As the seventeenth generation of a samurai family with strong cultural connections to Japan, the sisters' company offers a hybrid of traditional American and Japanese philosophy in instruction, choreography, and design.

Cathy Young

Since she joined The Boston Conservatory in 2011, **Cathy Young**'s leadership of the Dance Division has ushered in a period of unprecedented growth that only accelerated after the school's 2016 merger with Berklee.

In 2016, as Dean of Dance at Boston Conservatory at Berklee, Young hired **Duane Lee Holland, Jr.**—the first joint faculty appointment for the merged institution and the first faculty position in hip-hop dance—and established a program with the renowned Royal Academy of Dance that offers Conservatory students a ballet pedagogy credential, the first of its kind in the United States. Young has also taken the lead in developing a new jazz dance major that will expand Conservatory offerings.

Young's hiring marks only the fourth leadership change since **Jan Veen** founded the Dance Department (later called the Dance Division) in 1943. While the program

that Young inherited from the esteemed **Yasuko "Yasi" Tokunaga** is still rooted in classical training, it has embraced new styles and techniques, adapted cutting-edge technology, and pursued new collaborations both on campus and in the community.

Young's work has received widespread critical acclaim. In April 2016, *Backstage* credited The Boston Conservatory's dance program as being the best contemporary dance program in the United States. The performing arts news website OnStage.com ranked the Conservatory fourth on its list of the "Top 10 Dance Colleges in the Country" and also lauded the school's contemporary dance program as being "the best in the United States." And in July 2016, in an article titled "Dance Degrees, Rebooted," *Dance Magazine* acknowledged the program for the way it "prepares its dance students with courses focused on creating an online presence, self-producing, marketing and fundraising."

Young's successes can also be measured by faculty she has appointed, including alumnus and noted Límon instructor **Kurt Douglas** (B.F.A. '01, dance), and by the successes of recent graduates: **Charles Patterson** (B.F.A. '16, dance), member of Complexions Contemporary Ballet; **Kate Ladenheim** (B.F.A. '11, dance), creative director and choreographer for The People Movers Contemporary Dance; **Brent Sjoblom** (B.F.A. '12, dance), Nashville Ballet company member; **Lilian Balch** (B.F.A. '15, dance), dancer with Shen Wei Dance Arts; **Ariane Michaud** and **Katharina Schier** (both B.F.A. '16, dance), who launched the Conservatory's first Senior Dance Performance in New York City and secured it as an annual event; and **Holly Wilder** (B.F.A. '15, dance), cofounder the Wilder Project, an award-winning dance film company that exclusively features Conservatory dancers.

Ebony Williams

When contemporary dancer **Ebony Williams** (B.F.A. '05, dance) takes the stage, her freedom of movement makes it seem like anything is possible. A native of Boston's Dorchester neighborhood, Williams had her first dance lesson at the age of 8 at the Roxbury Center for the Performing Arts, where she earned a spot to train at the Boston Ballet's Citydance program. She went on to study at The Boston Conservatory and, shortly after, joined the Cedar Lake Contemporary Ballet in Brooklyn, New York, where she was a member for ten years before the company closed in 2015.

It was Cedar Lake that first brought Williams back to Boston as a professional dancer, to perform in a show at the Shubert Theatre that was being presented as part of the Celebrity Series of Boston. During her stay, Williams visited The Boston Conservatory's recently renovated facilities at 31 Hemenway Street. Impressed with the improvements, she told *Boston Magazine*: "We had the smallest little studios and a really rickety theater when I was [at the Conservatory], and now it is a beautiful building with windows everywhere, with amazing studios, and it's awesome."

Williams may be best known as one of two dancers accompanying **Beyoncé** in her blockbuster video *Single Ladies (Put a Ring on It)*. With its signature choreography, hand moves, and black-and-white cinematography, it is estimated to have been seen by more than one billion people worldwide. Williams performed again with Beyoncé in 2016, during the Super Bowl 50 Halftime Show.

Williams' success lies in her willingness to embrace diverse opportunities. She told a newspaper interviewer in 2015, "I'm just going to do everything I can do—everything that I didn't have time for, everything that is risky, everything that I'm afraid of. I want to jump in."

31 Hemenway Street

Nestled in a corner of a busy Boston neighborhood, 31 Hemenway Street's staid exterior belies the creativity and hard work that occurs in its many rehearsal and performances spaces. This hub of activity, which is a staple of the Conservatory community, went through a $30 million renovation known as the Hemenway Project. The project was completed in 2010, making the building a vital part of the school's campus.

The project added 16,000 square feet of much-needed space to the preexisting building, including the construction of a new theater studio, two large-volume dance studios, and a music rehearsal and performance space for large ensembles. It also allowed for the transformation of the Boston Conservatory Theater from a traditional auditorium to a state-of-the-art theater, including an orchestra pit, accessible seating, air conditioning, and new sound and lighting technology. This 325-seat mainstage theater serves as the home for all major performances by the Dance, Music, and Theater Divisions.

Alumni frequently reminisce about the building and the performance spaces as they existed during their time at the school. A consistent memory among dancers is the ever-present former Board of Trustees Chairman **Alfred D. Houston** and his wife, **Patricia**, at performances in the building. "We really have been fixtures at the performances, particularly anything from the Dance Division," Houston said. "I think that's why it was so important to us that the spaces in 31 Hemenway get the upgrade that was needed. [. . .] We heard from dancers how they could not rehearse in the studios without their partners hitting their heads in some rooms."

Houston was chairman during the Hemenway Project, and he sat proudly in his familiar seat for *Opening Note!*, the series of performances held to celebrate the reopening of the building in October 2010. The celebratory concert included performances by the Conservatory's premier ensemble, Hemenway Strings, as well as special guest and Tony Award–nominee **Chad Kimball** (B.F.A. '99, musical theater), known for his starring role in the Broadway musical, *Memphis*.

Houston credits the success of the Hemenway Project to his predecessor, Chairwoman **Mimi Hewlett**. Hewlett, a philanthropist who has supported a range of arts organizations, served on the Conservatory's board from 2001 to 2016 and championed the project with fierce dedication. While serving as president of the late Guild of the Opera Company of Boston, Hewlett described her conviction in a *Boston Globe* article: "Arts organizations are so fragile, but they must go on; they're vital."

The 2010 *Opening Note!* event was reminiscent of 31 Hemenway Street's original dedication and opening concerts in 1949, which occurred under Conservatory director **Albert Alphin**. That opening concert was heralded as "a joyous celebration" ten years in the making. It included performances by noted faculty members **Alvin Ball** (trumpet), **H. Wilfred Churchill** (piano), **Lucie Elcus** (piano), **Henri Girard** (double bass), **Edward Molitore** (tenor), the Boston Conservatory Honors String Quartet, and **Joseph Silverstein** (violin), who performed as a soloist with the Hemenway Strings.

Alphin had originally sought to acquire 31 Hemenway Street in the late 1930s, but World War II and wartime restrictions to the use of construction materials delayed the project. When 31 Hemenway finally opened in 1949, Alphin was well aware of its potential. "This [building]," he said, "is key to our future and our growth."

Houston Hall

Houston Hall, formerly the Concert Hall, was named for **Alfred D. Houston**, a past Chair of the Board of Trustees of Boston Conservatory, and his wife, **Patricia Houston**, for their contributions towards the building of 132 Ipswich Street. Known as "Al" by most, Houston was integral in stewarding many advancements on the Conservatory campus, including renovations to 31 Hemenway Street facility. He and his wife have been front-row ticket holders for nearly all mainstage performances during his tenure and also sponsor an annual named scholarship for two dance students, called the Al and Pat Houston Dance Scholarship.

As of 2017, Houston Hall continues to be a primary classroom space for current students and faculty. Its intimate setting and acoustics make it the favorite location for student recitals.

Top left: Alfred D. Houston; *Top right*: From left: Michael Morris, Jr. (B.F.A. '16, dance), Kelsey McCormack (B.F.A. '16, dance), Patricia Houston, and Alfred D. Houston

Pam Kunkemueller's Artists in Residence

Pam Kunkemueller's love of the performing arts is embodied in the artist residency program that she made possible at The Boston Conservatory. The program, which brings some of the best artists in their disciplines to the school, has enriched the Conservatory's world-class training and has inspired creativity on campus since 2008.

Kunkemueller, a donor whose gifts enabled construction of the Boston Conservatory Theater's orchestra pit, first got the idea for a guest artist program while attending a weekend of master classes at the Metropolitan Opera in New York City.

There, she was struck by how the students and guests responded to working with the professional artists brought in for the classes, she told *STAGES* magazine in 2015.

After a discussion with Conservatory president **Richard Ortner**, the Kunkemueller Artist Residency Program was born. Over the years, it has brought dozens of leading artists to the school, including composer **Louis Andriessen**, soprano **Tony Arnold**, Broadway star **Barbara Cook**, dancer **Peter DiMuro**, violinist **Jorja Fleezanis**, two-time Tony Award–winning composer **Adam Guettel**, and soprano **Dawn Upshaw**.

The program is curated by Conservatory deans, who work with faculty to invite acclaimed artists to campus to work with students in and out of the classroom through master classes, lectures, and performances.

Kunkemueller has since turned over the administration of the program to the Conservatory, but said that she attends master classes whenever she can. "I love to watch the process and be a fly on the wall," she said. "I am there to learn like everyone else. I love The Boston Conservatory, and it's thrilling to see that the program is actively making an impact."

Bottom: From left, Monica Germino, Richard Ortner, Pam Kunkemueller, and Louis Andriessen

Karl Paulnack's Welcome Address

What began as Music Division Director **Karl Paulnack**'s usual welcome address to the parents of the 2004 incoming music class quickly became a rallying cry for music and arts education that resounded well beyond the Boston Conservatory campus.

"[Music is] not a luxury, a lavish thing that we fund from leftovers of our budgets, not a plaything or an amusement or a pass time," Paulnack said. "Music is a basic need of human survival. Music is one of the ways we make sense of our lives, one of the ways in which we express feelings when we have no words, a way for us to understand things with our hearts when we can't with our minds."

Paulnack's words became an overnight sensation in the music world, and gained further prominence in 2009 when music legend **Linda Ronstadt** brought them to the attention of legislators in Washington, D.C. while advocating for arts funding in schools. In her March 31, 2009 testimony before the Congressional Committee on Arts Funding, Ronstadt quoted Paulnack, saying, "As renowned music educator Karl Paulnack, music director and conductor of the orchestra [sic] at the Boston

Conservatory, said about great music: 'It has the ability to crack your heart open like a walnut; it can make you cry over sadness you didn't know you had. Music can slip beneath our conscious reality to get at what's really going on inside us.'"

Paulnack's welcome speech to parents not only made a compelling case for arts education, but set the bar very high for Conservatory students. "Frankly, ladies and gentlemen, I expect you not only to master music, I expect you to save the planet," said Paulnack, who served as director of the Music Division from 2002 to 2013. "If there is to be a future of peace for humankind [...] I expect it will come from the artists, because that's what we do."

Paulnack, an established pianist, met Conservatory President Richard Ortner while a faculty member at the Tanglewood Music Center. Ortner was so impressed by the University of Minnesota School of Music alumnus that he created the first-ever adjunct faculty position for him at the Conservatory. After his tenure as music division director at the Conservatory, Paulnack was appointed dean of Ithaca College School of Music in 2013.

Welcome Address to the Incoming Class of 2004

One of my parents' deepest fears, I suspect, is that society would not properly value me as a musician, that I wouldn't be appreciated. I had very good grades in high school, I was good in science and math, and they imagined that as a doctor or a research chemist or an engineer, I might be more appreciated than I would be as a musician. I still remember my mother's remark when I announced my decision to apply to music school. She said, "You're wasting your SAT scores!"

On some level, I think, my parents were not sure themselves what the value of music was, what its purpose was. And they loved music: they listened to classical music all the time. They just weren't really clear about its function. So let me talk about that a little bit, because we live in a society that puts music in the "arts and entertainment" section of the newspaper, and serious music—the kind your kids are about to engage in—has absolutely nothing whatsoever to do with entertainment; in fact, it's the opposite of entertainment. Let me talk a little bit about music and how it works.

One of the first cultures to articulate how music really works were the ancient Greeks. And this is going to fascinate you: the Greeks said that music and astronomy were two sides of the same coin. Astronomy was seen as the study of relationships between observable, permanent, external objects, and music was seen as the study of relationships between invisible, internal, hidden objects. Music has a way of finding the big, invisible moving pieces inside our hearts and souls and helping us figure out the position of things inside us. Let me give you some examples of how this works.

One of the most profound musical compositions of all time is the *Quartet for the End of Time*, written by French composer Olivier Messiaen in 1940. Messiaen was 31 years old when France entered the war against Nazi Germany. He was captured by the Germans in June of 1940 and imprisoned in a prisoner-of-war camp.

He was fortunate to find a sympathetic prison guard who gave him paper and a place to compose, and fortunate to have musician colleagues in the camp: a cellist, a violinist, and a clarinetist. Messiaen wrote his quartet with these specific players in mind. It was performed in January 1941 for four thousand prisoners and guards in the prison camp. Today, it is one of the most famous masterworks in the repertoire.

Given what we have since learned about life in the Nazi camps, why would anyone in his right mind waste time and energy writing or playing music? There was barely enough energy on a good day to find food and water, to avoid a beating, to stay warm, to escape torture—why would anyone bother with music? And yet—even from the concentration camps—we have poetry, we have music, we have visual art; it wasn't just this one fanatic Messiaen; many, many people created art. Why? Well, in a place where people are only focused on survival, on the bare necessities, the obvious conclusion is that art must be, somehow, essential for life. The camps were without money, without hope, without commerce, without recreation, without basic respect, but they were not without art. Art is part of survival; art is part of the human spirit, an unquenchable expression of who we are. Art is one of the ways in which we say, "I am alive, and my life has meaning."

In September of 2001, I was a resident of Manhattan. On the morning of September 12, 2001, I reached a new understanding of my art and its relationship to the world. I sat down at the piano that morning at 10:00 a.m. to practice, as was my daily routine; I did it by force of habit, without thinking about it. I lifted the cover on the keyboard and opened my music, put my hands on the keys, and took my hands off the keys. And I sat there and thought, does this even matter? Isn't this completely irrelevant? Playing the piano right now, given what happened in this city yesterday, seems silly, absurd, irreverent, pointless. Why am I here? What place has a musician in this moment in time? Who needs a piano player right now? I was completely lost.

And then I, along with the rest of New York, went through the journey of getting through that week. I did not play the piano that day, and in fact I contemplated briefly whether I would ever want to play the piano again. And then I observed how we got through the day.

At least in my neighborhood, we didn't shoot hoops or play Scrabble. We didn't play cards to pass the time, we didn't watch TV, we didn't shop, we most certainly did not go to the mall. The first organized activity that I saw in New York, on the very evening of September 11, was singing. People sang. People sang around fire houses, people sang "We Shall Overcome." Lots of people sang "America the Beautiful." The first organized public event that I remember was the Brahms *Requiem,* later that week at Lincoln Center, with the New York Philharmonic. The first organized public expression of grief, our first communal response to that historic event, was a concert. That was the beginning of a sense that life might go on. The United States military secured the airspace, but recovery was led by the arts, and by music in particular, that very night.

From these two experiences, I have come to understand that music is not part of "arts and entertainment" as the newspaper section would have us believe. It's not a luxury, a lavish thing that we fund from leftovers of our budgets, not a plaything or an amusement or a pastime. Music is a basic need of human survival. Music is one of the ways we make sense of our lives, one of the ways in which we express feelings when we have no words, a way for us to understand things with our hearts when we can't with our minds.

Some of you may know Samuel Barber's heart wrenchingly beautiful piece, *Adagio for Strings.* If you don't know it by that name, then some of you may know it as the

background music which accompanied the Oliver Stone movie *Platoon,* a film about the Vietnam War. If you know that piece of music either way, you know it has the ability to crack your heart open like a walnut; it can make you cry over sadness you didn't know you had. Music can slip beneath our conscious reality to get at what's really going on inside us, the way a good therapist does.

Very few of you have ever been to a wedding where there was absolutely no music. There might have been only a little music, there might have been some really bad music, but with few exceptions there is some music. And something very predictable happens at weddings—people get all pent up with all kinds of emotions, and then there's some musical moment where the action of the wedding stops and someone sings or plays the flute or something. And even if the music is lame, even if the quality isn't good, predictably 30 or 40 percent of the people who are going to cry at a wedding cry a couple of moments after the music starts. Why? The Greeks. Music allows us to move around those big invisible pieces of ourselves and rearrange our insides so that we can express what we feel even when we can't talk about it. Can you imagine watching *Indiana Jones* or *Superman* or *Star Wars* with the dialogue but no music? What is it about the music swelling up at just the right moment in *E.T.* so that all the softies in the audience start crying at exactly the same moment? I guarantee you if you showed the movie with the music stripped

out, it wouldn't happen that way. The Greeks. Music is the understanding of the relationship between invisible internal objects.

I'll give you one more example, the story of the most important concert of my life. I must tell you, I have played a little less than a thousand concerts in my life so far. I have played in places that I thought were important. I like playing in Carnegie Hall; I enjoyed playing in Paris; it made me very happy to please the critics in St. Petersburg. I have played for people I thought were important; music critics of major newspapers, foreign heads of state. The most important concert of my entire life took place in a nursing home in a small Midwestern town a few years ago.

I was playing with a very dear friend of mine who is a violinist. We began, as we often do, with Aaron Copland's Sonata, which was written during World War II and dedicated to a young friend of Copland's, a young pilot who was shot down during the war. Now we often talk to our audiences about the pieces we are going to play rather than providing them with written program notes. But in this case, because we began the concert with this piece, we decided to talk about the piece later in the program and to just come out and play the music without explanation.

Midway through the piece, an elderly man seated in a wheelchair near the front of the concert hall began to weep.

This man, whom I later met, was clearly a soldier—even in his 70s, it was clear from his buzz-cut hair, square jaw, and general demeanor that he had spent a good deal of his life in the military. I thought it a little bit odd that someone would be moved to tears by that particular movement of that particular piece, but it wasn't the first time I've heard crying in a concert, and we went on with the concert and finished the piece.

When we came out to play the next piece on the program, we decided to talk about both the first and second pieces, and we described the circumstances in which the Copland was written and mentioned its dedication to a downed pilot. The man in the front of the audience became so disturbed that he had to leave the auditorium. I honestly figured that we would not see him again, but he did come backstage afterwards, tears and all, to explain himself.

What he told us was this: "During World War II, I was a pilot, and I was in an aerial combat situation where one of my team's planes was hit. I watched my friend bail out, and watched his parachute open, but the Japanese planes which had engaged us returned and machine gunned across the parachute cords so as to separate the parachute from the pilot, and I watched my friend drop away into the ocean, realizing that he was lost. I have not thought about this for many years, but during that first piece of music you played, this memory returned to me so vividly that it was as

though I was reliving it. I didn't understand why this was happening, why now, but then when you came out to explain that this piece of music was written to commemorate a lost pilot, it was a little more than I could handle. How does the music do that? How did it find those feelings and those memories in me?"

Remember the Greeks: Music is the study of invisible relationships between internal objects. The concert in the nursing home was the most important work I have ever done. For me to play for this old soldier and help him connect, somehow, with Aaron Copland, and to connect their memories of their lost friends, to help him remember and mourn his friend, this is my work. This is why music matters.

What follows is part of the talk I will give to this year's freshman class when I welcome them a few days from now. The responsibility I will charge your sons and daughters with is this:

If we were a medical school, and you were here as a med student practicing appendectomies, you'd take your work very seriously because you would imagine that some night at 2:00 a.m. someone is going to waltz into your emergency room and you're going to have to save their life. Well, my friends, someday at 8:00 p.m. someone is going to walk into your concert hall and bring you a mind that is confused, a heart that is overwhelmed, a soul that is weary. Whether they go out whole again

will depend partly on how well you do your craft.

You're not here to become an entertainer, and you don't have to sell yourself. The truth is you don't have anything to sell; being a musician isn't about dispensing a product, like selling used cars. I'm not an entertainer; I'm a lot closer to a paramedic, a firefighter, a rescue worker. You're here to become a sort of therapist for the human soul, a spiritual version of a chiropractor, physical therapist, someone who works with our insides to see if they get things to line up, to see if we can come into harmony with ourselves and be healthy and happy and well.

Frankly, ladies and gentlemen, I expect you not only to master music; I expect you to save the planet. If there is a future wave of wellness on this planet, of harmony, of peace, of an end to war, of mutual understanding, of equality, of fairness, I don't expect it will come from a government, a military force, or a corporation. I no longer even expect it to come from the religions of the world, which together seem to have brought us as much war as they have peace. If there is a future of peace for humankind, if there is to be an understanding of how these invisible, internal things should fit together, I expect it will come from the artists, because that's what we do. As in the concentration camp and the evening of 9/11, the artists are the ones who might be able to help us with our internal, invisible lives.

Music Education

Boston Conservatory established its Music Education Department in 1933, offering a diploma in "Public School Music." In 1938, it became the first conservatory to offer a degree in music education and, years later, the school added graduate-level degrees with concentrations in music education and autism. With autism as its unique area of concentration, the Boston Conservatory program quickly rose to be a top program in the country.

Led by **Rhoda Bernard**, Ed.D. since 2004, and (as of fall 2017) housed under the Berklee's Institute for Arts Education and Special Needs, the Conservatory's music education programs render close to 100-percent job placement and boast groundbreaking outreach programs for children on the autism spectrum and their families.

In 2015, the Massachusetts Cultural Council awarded the Conservatory a prestigious Commonwealth Award in the category of Access for "its groundbreaking work on making the arts accessible to everyone." Upon accepting the award, Conservatory President **Richard Ortner** said, "The program for students with autism is a leading example for both the world of higher education and the arts community at large. Community inclusion is part of The Boston Conservatory's DNA, and this honor is wonderful validation of that mission."

Abra K. Bush

Abra K. Bush came to the Conservatory from the Eastman School of Music at the University of Rochester. An acknowledged expert in the field of assessment, Bush led a significant curricular review, immediately focusing on the creation and presentation of new works as one of the hallmarks of the program.

Bush strengthened the school's annual New Music Festival and invited extraordinary soprano **Tony Arnold** to become the 2015–2016 Kunkemueller Artist in Residence. She also instituted a master's degree program in contemporary music performance, led by Woodwind Department Chair **Michael Norsworthy**. Focusing on music written after 1950, the program attracts instrumentalists and singers with the special skills and extended technique required to do advanced work— directly with composers—on the latest in new music. Bush, the first vocalist to lead the Music Division, was also a frequent performer while at the Conservatory. Working with cellist Rhonda Rider and seven other Conservatory cellists, Bush gave memorable performances of Villa Lobos' beloved *Bachianas Brasilieras*, No. 5.

Bush earned her bachelor of music in voice performance and master of music in opera theater from Oberlin College's Conservatory of Music and completed her doctorate of musical arts in voice at Ohio State University School of Music. She left the Conservatory in March 2016 to pursue the position of senior associate dean at The Peabody Institute of The John Hopkins University.

Right, from top: Tony Arnold, Michael Norsworthy, and Abra K. Bush with Lawrence Isaacson

Gianna Hitsos and the Programs for Students on the Autism Spectrum

"Everyone was so nice. That was a total change," **Gianna Hitsos** said of The Boston Conservatory's Program for Students on the Autism Spectrum, which trains musically talented students on the autism spectrum, ages 9 and older. "They didn't see me as an autistic kid. Once they heard me sing, they were like, 'Whoa!'"

In 2009, Hitsos enrolled in the Conservatory's weekly private music lesson program—the first conservatory-level program in the United States to pair students on the autism spectrum with music education graduate students. She credits it with helping her get through high school and into Gordon College.

"Music has always helped me process things better, but it has turned into so much more," Hitsos wrote on her guest blog for the nonprofit organization Autism Speaks.

The Conservatory, too, has seen the changes in the autistic students that participate in this innovative program. "We have a population here that has always heard about their deficits," said **Rhoda Bernard**, Ed.D., the Conservatory administrator who oversees the program, in a *Boston Globe* column by **Thomas Farragher**. "We want to show them what they can do."

Like others in the program, Hitsos's Conservatory training has unlocked new opportunities that have helped her establish herself as a professional singer. In 2013, she sang *God Bless America* at Fenway Park during a Red Sox game; in 2015, she performed at the gala for the Commonwealth Awards, Massachusetts' highest honor in arts, humanities, and sciences, which recognized the Conservatory's autism program that year; and on June 20, 2016, she sang at the Broadway Benefit for Autism Speaks at the Gershwin Theatre in New York City.

Top: Boston Conservatory opera singers perform for students at the Boston Higashi School in Randolph, Massachusetts, 2015;
Bottom: Rhoda Bernard, Ed.D., and Gianna Hitsos at the Massachusetts Cultural Council Commonwealth Award Ceremony, 2015

Wang Meng Ngee

Wang Meng Ngee's (M.M. '96, double bass) life has been an adventure—first in music, and then as a world traveler.

After completing her dual master's degree in music performance (double bass) and music education at the Conservatory in December of 1997, Wang remained in Boston for six years working as a teacher at the Windsor School in Boston, Cambridge Public Schools, and Boston Public Schools. She also worked as a freelance performer with the Boston Philharmonic Orchestra and other regional orchestras, as well as with a string trio at private events.

In 2001, she met her husband, **Franck Ibanez**, whose dream was to sail around the world. They realized that dream together, when Wang was invited back to her hometown to join the Singapore Symphony Orchestra as staff and the Singapore Chinese Orchestra as principal bass.

They remained in Singapore for twelve years, until their taste for adventure again flared, and they packed their bags, this time with their two young daughters, **Carmen** and **Julie**. In 2013, the family moved to Hong Kong, where the girls are students at the Hong Kong French International School and where Wang works as the school's music teacher.

"The training I had [at the Conservatory] has made me a very flexible professional musician. I am not a slave to just one category of music job in particular," Wang wrote in an email sent from Hong Kong. "My teachers had been such great role models that it did not take me long to understand that if I am out there teaching or performing, I have to have fun but also be responsible, on time, and serious."

Nate Tucker

Percussionist **Nate Tucker** (B.M. '12, percussion) has launched a successful career in musical theater, and his early career path has been defined not only by his talent, but also by his creativity and his drive.

"As a musician and a composer, Nate is a great example of the artistic curiosity and collaborative energy that is at the heart of the Contemporary Theater program," said **Wanda Strukus**, then director of the Conservatory's contemporary theater program. Strukus had invited Tucker back to the Conservatory in 2015 as a guest lecturer for her students, calling him "a great role model" for contemporary theater students because of his "proactive approach to his career."

Tucker's local credits include stints as music director for Mount Auburn Cemetery's *A Glimpse Beyond*, principal percussionist for Juventas New Music Ensemble and Flamenco Boston, resident composer for the Boston Theater Company, Come On Over Ensemble Theater, and Danza Organica, and accompanist for the Boston Ballet and the Conservatory.

Tucker also has established a reputation as a performer. In the American Repertory Theater's (A.R.T.) 2014 production of *The Tempest*, Tucker was part of an onstage band that performed the music of **Tom Waits**. Tucker returned to the A.R.T. later that same year as part of the *Finding Neverland* orchestra and again in 2015 to perform in *Natasha, Pierre & The Great Comet of 1812*, both of which later opened on Broadway.

Awards and Honors

Boston Conservatory students, alumni, and faculty have been honored with some of the most prestigious awards and honors that the arts industry has to offer.

In 2016, **Jennifer Simard** (B.F.A. '92, musical theater) was nominated for a Tony Award for her show-stopping performance as a nun with a gambling addiction in *Disaster!*, a comic send-up of 1970s disaster films, in the Best Featured Actress in a Musical category.

Ben Simpson (B.F.A. '11, musical theater) and **Joe Longthorne** (B.F.A. '12, musical theater) were among the credited producers who shared the Best Musical Tony Award for *Waitress*, an adaptation of the 2007 movie. The acclaimed Broadway production, which opened in April 2016, also starred former Conservatory student **Kimiko Glenn**, best known for her role in the hit Netflix series, *Orange Is the New Black*. (Glenn left the Conservatory in her freshman year after being cast as Thea in the first national tour of *Spring Awakening*.)

That same show marked the 2016 return to the Tony Awards for **Constantine Maroulis** (B.F.A. '02, musical theater), who was part of the producing team that received the Best Revival nomination for mounting Deaf West Theater's production of *Spring Awakening* on Broadway. The show was celebrated as historic for bringing deaf and hearing actors together on the same stage and for seamlessly merging American Sign Language into the show. In 2009, Maroulis was nominated for Best Performance of a Leading Actor in a Musical for his portrayal of Drew in *Rock of Ages*.

The alumnus with the greatest Tony success is the late **Thommie Walsh**, a 1972 Conservatory graduate who was nominated for four Tony Awards. His two wins came for choreography for collaborating with **Tommy Tune** in 1980 on *A Day in Hollywood/A Night in the Ukraine* and in 1983 on *My One and Only*, in which Tune starred. History, however, best remembers Walsh for creating the role of Bobby in *A Chorus Line*.

Chad Kimball (B.F.A. '99, musical theater) was nominated in 2010 for Best Actor in a Musical for *Memphis*, in which he portrayed Huey Calhoun, a role he originated. Kimball, who returned to the Conservatory for the reopening of 31 Hemenway Street after its $30 million renovation, appeared in the 2002 Broadway revival of Stephen Sondheim's *Into the Woods* and the Broadway productions of *Lennon* and *Good Vibrations*.

Faculty members have also received Tony recognition. **Maureen Brennan**, a musical theater faculty member, was nominated in 1974 for her Broadway debut as Cunégonde in *Candide*. And, **Patsy Collins Bandes**, the Conservatory's production stage manager and theater faculty member, was the stage manager of the Denver Center Theatre Company when it won the Regional Theatre Tony Award in 1998. While in Denver, Collins Bandes worked on the world premieres of *The Laramie Project* and *Give 'em a Bit of Mystery: Shakespeare and the Old Tradition*.

Chad Kimball

Mike McGrath

Lorraine Hunt Lieberson

Beyond the Tonys, Conservatory alumna and Metropolitan Opera performer **Lorraine Hunt Lieberson**, heralded as one of the greatest mezzo-sopranos of her generation, posthumously received the Grammy Award for Best Classical Vocal Performance for the recording of *Rilke Songs*, written by her husband, **Peter Lieberson**. She won again in 2008 for her performance of her husband's *Neruda Songs*.

Conservatory alumnus and actor **Mike McGrath** (B.F.A. '76, musical theater) has more than a dozen Broadway credits to his name, including *Spamalot*, which brought him a Tony Award nomination

in 2005, and *Nice Work If You Can Get It*, for which he won the Tony Award for Best Featured Actor in a Musical in 2012. McGrath is a Worcester native who met his wife, actress **Toni DiBuono**, when they were performing in *Forbidden Broadway* in Boston. The couple later worked together in the Broadway revival of *Wonderful Town*.

The Conservatory also counts a Newbery Medal–winning author among its alumni. **Elizabeth Borton de Trevino** studied violin at the school in the late 1920s after graduating from Stanford University with a degree in Latin American history. After marrying, she moved to Mexico and had two sons. Her older son, **Luis**, and his

interest in art inspired her book, *I, Juan de Pareja*, through his interest in art. The book, published in 1965, is about the artist **Diego Velázquez** and his slave **Juan de Pareja**, who modeled for the painter. In 1966, de Trevino was awarded the Newbery Medal, given annually by the American Library Association for a book that made the "most distinguished contribution to American literature for children."

A last notable achievement is composer **Roger Sessions**, who won two Pulitzer Prizes for his music several decades after he taught in Boston.

The Years to Come

2016 and Beyond

Quality comes first.

Throughout its 150-year history, despite its ups and downs, Boston Conservatory has maintained an unwavering dedication to its students and the quality of instruction it provides. While this commitment has been present since its founding, it has evolved throughout the school's history to mean so much more, not only for the students and communities it serves, but also for the performing arts in general.

As the Conservatory embarks on its next 150 years, the story of the Conservatory's future is ready to be written. With the game-changing alliance with Berklee in 2016 and a shared vision for boundless creation, the Conservatory is undoubtedly poised to achieve whatever its imagination can conjure.

In this section, we explore some of the projects and people that we believe capture the boldness and creativity that will define the future of the Conservatory and the future of the arts. While we cannot say exactly what the next 150 years will bring, we are confident that our students will lead the way, embodying the Conservatory's unwavering spirit and drive for innovation.

132 Ipswich Street

The gleaming glass façade at 132 Ipswich Street is the most modern example of the Boston Conservatory's physical presence at the vanguard of performing arts education.

The 20,000-square-foot building includes classrooms, dance studios, multipurpose studios, a performance library, a large orchestra rehearsal hall, and teaching studios. The first building that the Conservatory constructed from scratch, 132 Ipswich Street formally opened in September 2014 and has been a vibrant, creative space ever since.

"It's about synthesis," said Conservatory President **Richard Ortner**. "I believe it's vital that music, dance, and theater students encounter each other hourly, informally—to learn how work is made in disciplines other than their own. It's part of what's special about the Conservatory. The beauty—indeed, the intent—of the 132 Ipswich Street building is that those 'collisions' are baked into the way the building functions. Students and faculty experience that immersion, which in turn allows them to think and create together. It enhances artistic literacy in ways that expand the idea of what is possible." The creation of the collaborative environment

at 132 Ipswich was a highlight of Ortner's administration.

The location of the building, in clear view from the Massachusetts Turnpike, makes it a highly visible presence for all of the traffic coming into and going out of the city, bringing the Conservatory a modern architectural prominence that rivals Boston's other institutions of higher education.

"When we opened the building, I was struck by how 132 Ipswich would be seen by others, the many cars—including my own—that commute on the Pike," said **David Scott Sloan**, most recent chairman of the Boston Conservatory Board of Trustees. "Now that a couple of years have passed, I also realize how it has let us expand the Conservatory's view of what we do and how it fits into the city and beyond."

Ortner credits the trustees, particularly former board chairs **Alfred D. Houston** and **Mimi Hewlett**, with making the project a reality. "It was the vision of those who made constructing a new building possible, coming so soon after the 2010 renovation and expansion of 31 Hemenway," said Ortner.

That sentiment was echoed by longtime trustee **Anthony Pangaro**, who said that the chance to buy the lot and build the facility was a once-in-a-lifetime opportunity. "Schools should be precious places for learning, and a lot of learning occurs in the spaces between the programmed rooms of a building like [132 Ipswich Street]," Pangaro said. "The building's appearance will also help people to understand what we do here, and how to approach it."

The community's response was immediate and positive, both for the building and the work that goes on inside.

"The Boston Conservatory is an important part of the thriving Fenway neighborhood, next door to the Boston Arts Academy, and its expansion creates many additional opportunities for its talented students," said United States Representative **Michael E. Capuano** (D-MA 7th District). "And this new building not only expands the Conservatory's campus, but it allows the Conservatory to grow its capacity to educate students and give them unparalleled opportunities."

The Merger of The Boston Conservatory and Berklee

In June 2015, The Boston Conservatory and Berklee College of Music made a sensational announcement: the two institutions had entered a Memorandum of Understanding to formally explore a merger. The prospect was groundbreaking. If it went through, it would be the first time in known history that two independent performing arts schools joined forces to set a new global standard for performing arts training.

"The combined institution creates, in one stroke, the most comprehensive training ground for performing arts and related careers in the country, if not the world," Conservatory President **Richard Ortner** said of the potential merger at the time of the announcement.

For the next six months, the two schools worked together closely to determine whether or not a merger would benefit the student experience and the school's quality of training. The ultimate goal, as expressed by Berklee President **Roger H. Brown** and Conservatory President Richard Ortner, was to expand academic and artistic opportunities for all students and redefine performance training for the 21st-century artist.

By December 2015, the benefits had become clear, and both schools' governing boards voted unanimously to approve the merger. The merger legally went into effect on June 1, 2016, creating Boston Conservatory at Berklee.

"This merger was a bold step into the future of performing arts education," said **David Scott Sloan**, most recent chairman of The Boston Conservatory Board of Trustees, who led the team that structured the merger over the course of one year. "By bringing together the superb performing arts disciplines of The Boston Conservatory and Berklee, we have provided a unique platform that enables our students to draw upon global cultures and cutting-edge technologies as they synthesize completely new art forms. The Conservatory has been pioneering music, dance, and theater education for 150 years, and as part of the new Berklee, we continue to advance our mission as a dynamic institution that provides students with access to worldwide opportunities in performance and related fields that is without peer."

In the merged institution, the mission of Boston Conservatory at Berklee, as laid out by founder **Julius Eichberg** in 1867, remains intact. "Our goal is threefold," Brown said at the time that the merger was approved. "We want to attract the most talented, creative, and motivated students in the world; offer them a challenging, cutting-edge experience; and give them the best possible chance to succeed as professionals in a variety of careers."

In a 2016 podcast hosted by Massachusetts Cultural Council executive director **Anita Walker** and featuring Brown and Ortner, Ortner remarked, "There's a great cognate on our side: our students. Conservatory students are the ones who are taking the deepest possible dive into perfection of their craft, but they're less well-equipped to get it out there without a YouTube video, and Berklee's long and deep expertise in production, technology, engineering, and today in all—everything having to do with the digital realm—is

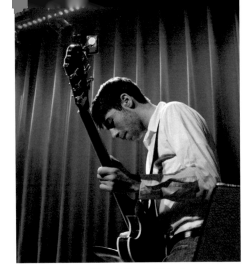

Left: Conservatory dancers in Karole Armitage's *Rave*, 2014; *Center*: Berklee College of Music student on electric guitar; *Right*: Conservatory cellist Nathaniel Taylor performs with the Boston Conservatory Orchestra, 2016

exactly what our students need in order to move them to the next level of career preparedness."

When the merger was announced, much attention was focused on how to elevate each school's most promising programs, such as jazz and rock (at Berklee) and dance and musical theater (at the Conservatory), while building upon programs that are complementary, such as Berklee's music therapy program and the Conservatory's music education in autism program.

The merger would also allow for the creation of more Conservatory summer and study abroad programs at Berklee's campus in Valencia, Spain, and—down the line—for Conservatory faculty members to develop courses for Berklee Online, which is already the world's largest and longest-running online music school, offering a bachelor's degree program, nearly 200 unique music courses, and more than 20 massive online open courses (MOOCs).

Though the merger naturally met with questions from constituents concerned about Berklee's considerably larger size (about seven times that of the Conservatory), the decision was overwhelmingly well-received by the Conservatory and Berklee communities, who found the benefits of a combined institution to be energizing and game-changing.

Additionally, many were already convinced of the advantages because of the many ways in which Berklee and the Conservatory have successfully worked together in the past. Over the course of their shared forty-six-year history, the neighboring institutions have shared faculty, shared food services, bought and sold Boston properties, and made use of each other's rehearsal and performance spaces. And for decades, Boston Conservatory and Berklee students have collaborated informally, as seen with the Berklee Indian Ensemble, the Neapolitan Orchestra, and the Berklee Silent Film Orchestra.

As part of the merger agreement, eight trustees from the Conservatory joined Berklee's forty-three-member Board of Trustees. The Conservatory's Board of Overseers, a voluntary group that acts to strengthen the Conservatory's connection to the community, remains fully functional and continues to provide expertise and consulting on special projects, and serving as representatives of the Conservatory. The new governance structure of the merged institution also includes a Leadership Council, which consists of legacy Conservatory Board Trustees who can represent the interests of the Conservatory to the combined board for consideration.

The 2016 merger was not the first time that the Conservatory considered possible partnerships or mergers. When **William A. Seymour** took the helm of the Conservatory in 1981 after a period of financial and academic instability, he twice looked at possible mergers, but found alternative solutions.

Aligning with the Conservatory's 150th anniversary in 2017, the merger with Berklee marks a period of rejuvenation for the Conservatory, as students, faculty, and staff begin to envision—and plan—a promising new future.

Longtime Friends

Pre-Merger Collaborations between
The Boston Conservatory and Berklee College of Music

Decades before the 2016 merger of The Boston Conservatory and Berklee, the two schools were already collaborating.

According to school records, when **William A. Seymour** first arrived at the Conservatory as an instructor in 1967, the school's faculty had been teaching music education classes for Berklee. "It was done for a few years before they asked me to teach those classes," Seymour said.

That same year, at the Conservatory's one hundredth anniversary celebration, the Conservatory's director, **Albert Alphin**, announced his retirement and indicated that **George A. Brambilla**, then dean of the Conservatory, would run the school. (From 1960 to 1963, Brambilla had been dean at Berklee College of Music, then called Berklee School of Music.)

In 1983, a handful of Boston arts schools joined forces and launched the Pro Arts Consortium, helping set the stage for collaborations between students at the Conservatory and Berklee. For the next two decades, Conservatory and Berklee students worked with each other on independent projects, and by the 2000s, Conservatory students were crossregistering for select Berklee classes.

Furthering their efforts to bring the arts together in Boston, Conservatory President **Richard Ortner** and Berklee President **Roger H. Brown** help to found the Boston Arts Academy (BAA)—Boston's public high school for visual and performing arts—in 1998. Today, Brown and Ortner remain key partners in BAA's growth and development.

In addition, many faculty members have taught at both the Conservatory and Berklee, including:

Elizabeth Allison, music education
Larry Bell, composition
Dana Brayton, orchestration, computer music, and ear training
John Coffey, trombone
Peter Cokkinias, wind ensemble, clarinet, and conducting

Left: Marimbist Nancy Zeltzman with a student; *Top right*: Composer Jonathan Bailey Holland; *Bottom*: Composer Marti Epstein

Wesley Copplestone, voice, oratory, and vocal literature

Harold Doyle, violin and string ensemble

Marti Epstein, composition

John Faieta, trombone

Susan Hagen, double bass

Jonathan Bailey Holland, composition

Kathleen Howland, music and cognition

Stefani Langol, music education

Alfred Lee, piano, solfeggio, and German

Lillian Lee, voice

Sharan Levanthal, violin

Everett Longstreth, arranging

Brian O'Connell, music education

Andrea Olmstead, music history, and Collegium Musicum

Walter Pavasaris, music education

Margaret Phillips, bassoon

Pasquale Prencipe, woodwinds and saxophone

Ali Ross, theater

Mary Saunders, voice

Kathryn Wright, voice

Nancy Zeltsman, percussion/marimba

A number of Conservatory alumni have also taught at Berklee, including: **Paul Schmeling**, who upon graduation in 1963 joined the theory faculty and would later teach ear training and serve as longtime chair of the Piano Department at Berklee. **Robert Fritz** (M.M. '68, composition) taught theory and composition from 1973 to 1975. **Gregory Fritze** (B.M. '76,

composition) joined the faculty in 1980, teaching trombone and composition, a position he still held in 2016. And, **Deanna Kidd Szymczak** (M.M. '76, music education) taught music education from 1977 to 2007.

Once the merger proceedings were underway in January 2016, the schools announced the first joint hire, **Duane Lee Holland, Jr.**, in May 2016. Holland is the Conservatory's first full-time faculty member teaching hip-hop dance. His classes and role were tailored to serve both Conservatory and Berklee students.

Fusing Art and Technology

As technology evolves, Boston Conservatory students are embracing what is new in order to push the boundaries of their art.

For her senior dance project, **Key'Aira Lockett** (B.F.A. '16, contemporary dance) conceptualized and choreographed a new work to original music composed specially for the dance by **Marc Hoffeditz** (P.S.C. '15, M.M. '14, composition), who studied with **Marti Epstein**. Lockett's choreography was incorporated projections from a Massachusetts College of Art and Design exhibit, making the piece a medley of art and technology.

Lockett is a native of Dallas, Texas, where she excelled as a dancer and made a name for herself through the Dallas Black Dance Theatre, from which she won a full scholarship to study at Boston Conservatory.

Katie Lynch's (B.F.A. '11, musical theater) performance skills and love for theater led her to a unique calling: she made her mark in the industry almost instantly after launching her webseries, *Backstage Bite*, for leading theater website BroadwayWorld.com. Lynch's first five segments debuted in May 2016 with a star-studded lineup, including an interview with Conservatory alumna **Kimiko Glenn**, who landed a leading role in the 2016 Tony Award–nominated musical *Waitress*.

Matt Rodin (B.F.A. '14, musical theater) is an actor whose creativity goes beyond the stage. Embracing his love for identity-building and design, Rodin has established a lucrative career working with other artists on branding and marketing. Most recently, he struck a deal with Playbill.com to turn his self-produced podcast series into a regular gig for the popular theater website, and has expanded his programming to cover everything from original sketches to Tony Award red-carpet coverage.

Taylor Rodman (B.F.A. '16, contemporary dance) collaborated with musicians from Berklee College of Music throughout her studies at the Conservatory as a dance major with an emphasis in creating performance. On several dance pieces that she created, she worked with composer **Jeff Kinsey**. Kinsey, a music production and engineering major who graduated from Berklee in 2014, created the music for her junior piece, "Below the Belt." While Rodman often choreographed her works based on the chosen music track, as is "the norm," it wasn't long before she began experimenting with choreographing a piece entirely without sound, and then composing music specially for the movement. This break with tradition resulted in a piece that was more powerful than Rodman had ever imagined.

"My entire experience at the Conservatory has been about exploration," Rodman said in an interview shortly before the 2016 commencement exercises. "Having arrived at the school with a strong background and interest in choreography, the Conservatory has been the perfect place for me to continue to develop my artistic voice."

Bottom left: Key'Aira Lockett; *Right:* Taylor Rodman

Marissa Rae Roberts and ToUch Performing Arts

Boston Conservatory alumna **Marissa Rae Roberts** (M.F.A. '12, musical theater) has made it her mission to change how the public thinks about theater.

Roberts, with her coartistic director, **Elizabeth McGuire** (B.F.A. '11, contemporary dance) established ToUch Performance Art, a production company based in Boston and New York dedicated to the creation and production of artistic works that provide immersive experiences, allowing audiences to experience theater in a personal, interactive way. ToUch's production *AcousticaElectronica*, which blends elements of electronic and classical

music, dance, circus arts, and immersive theater with the infectious energy of a nightclub, was in residence at the American Repertory Theater's second stage Oberon in Cambridge from 2013 to 2016.

Roberts' time at The Boston Conservatory taught her how to create meaningful performances and gave her the opportunity to hone her skills outside of the classroom. "I had great relationships with the incredible faculty and my extremely talented classmates," Roberts said. "I've had the opportunity to gain knowledge and experience from our collaborations, which has helped me to grow as an artist."

Musical Theater Showcase

For many prospective theater students at the Conservatory, the promise of the senior-year New York City showcase is a huge selling point. The showcase—which highlights the talent of the graduating class in front of a live audience of agents and casting companies—is an opportunity gain exposure in the industry as students prepare to make the leap into the professional world.

When Dean of Theater **Neil Donohoe** held the Conservatory's inaugural showcase in the 1980s, it was the first of its kind. "When we launched our in-person showcase, no one else was doing it—we were on the cutting edge," said Donohoe. Since then, the concept has become the industry standard among performing arts schools.

In 2016, the Theater Division introduced a new way to showcase performing arts students to industry professionals. The new model, called a "webcase," was a personalized, online performance portfolio and served as an extension of the in-person showcase. The Conservatory's first-ever webcase debuted in spring 2016 and featured video clips, headshots, and resume information for each of the seventy-one seniors of the graduate and undergraduate musical theater programs.

"The webcase is a new concept for performing arts schools, but the advantages [of an online presence] are so clear, I've no doubt that this will become the norm," said Donohoe.

For many students, the webcase also offered unexpected benefits. "Preparing to film the videos for the webcase gave me a new skillset that will be invaluable as I build a modern career in theater," said **Sara Gallo** (B.F.A. '16, musical theater), 2015–2016 president of the Student Government Association. "Learning these skills is so important because the industry is becoming more dependent on digital media."

In 2017, the showcase has evolved again, this time employing a hybrid model of the live NYC showcase with the webcase—or online actor database—as a supporting component. This model not only affords students and agents the ability to interface in person, but also allows agents who cannot attend the showcase, or may want to revisit student information, online access at any time. Showcase producer and longtime musical theater faculty member **Fran Charnas** lauded the students' embrace of the new platform as key to their success. "Our students are resourceful and flexible," she said. "That's what it takes to be in this business."

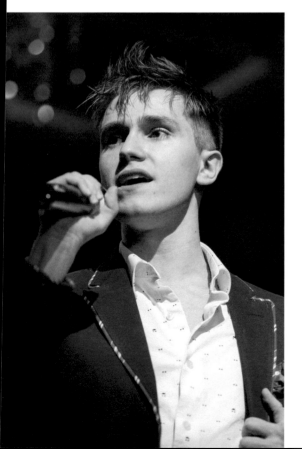

Partnership with Royal Academy of Dance

Boston Conservatory at Berklee is the first higher education arts institution in North America to offer students a ballet teaching credential in partnership with the Royal Academy of Dance (RAD) of London, the global leader for professional development in dance instruction and performance.

Slated to begin in May 2017, the partnership will allow Boston Conservatory students to earn RAD Registered Teacher Status once they complete both online coursework and an in-person practical module, which will be taught at the Conservatory.

"I think it is fair to say that the Royal Academy is the most recognized dance teacher accrediting body in the world, known for the excellence and depth of its pedagogy and teacher training," said **Cathy Young**, dean of dance at the Conservatory. "This gives our students not only access to an incredible wealth of knowledge about teaching dance, but also a certification that will allow them to find work anywhere in the world."

Students in the RAD Access Route program will complete the online portion of their coursework during the school year. The practical module will be taught during the summer in Boston by instructor **Gemma Williams**, one of two Royal Academy–trained teachers at Boston Conservatory. In the future, Young hopes that students will also have the opportunity to complete the practical module in London at the Royal Academy. "In the careers of twenty-first-century dance artists, teaching and performing are intertwined," Young said. "This program offers our students the unique opportunity to prepare themselves as world class teachers while also becoming world class performing artists."

"I really believe that to be a great teacher, you must be continually learning," Young said. "Teaching shows you what you don't know, and when our students train as teachers it gives them the ability to continually investigate what they are doing as performers."

Lower right: Gemma Williams

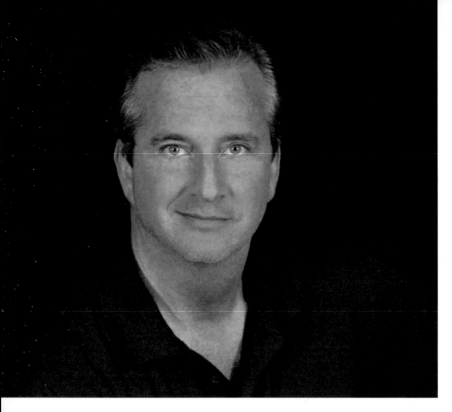

Sean Murphy

Growing up in Northern Ireland, **Sean Murphy** (B.F.A. '94, M.F.A. '96, dance) had to convince his childhood teacher **Mary Glaze**—who had classes brimming with young girls—to let him join the lessons. Now, through his own teaching, the Boston Conservatory alumnus makes it his mission to offer young people, particularly boys, a chance to express themselves through dance.

When Murphy arrived in the United States in 1987, he studied in New York City with the respected modern dancers and choreographers **Alwin Nikolais** and **Murray Louis**. He later moved to Boston and began his training at the Conservatory, where he received a B.F.A. and an M.F.A. in dance. He continues to support the Conservatory as a guest instructor, donor, and member of the school's Board of Overseers.

Today, Murphy shares his passion for dance as a teacher at the Eliot School, a kindergarten through eighth grade public school in Boston's North End, where he also oversees an internship program he established in 2010 to bring Boston Conservatory dance pedagogy students into the classroom. Murphy has also taught dance in the Lawrence and Medford public schools in Massachusetts.

Jennifer Scanlon, former principal dancer with José Limón Dance Company and dance instructor at the Conservatory, told *Dance Teacher Magazine* that Murphy's imagination makes him a great teacher—in addition to his boundless energy and passion. "What I think is amazing is that he teaches history and art, and he connects everything. He gets the kids involved in

their heritage and themselves," she told the magazine.

For Murphy, teaching dance to children is less about refining technique than it is about making it playful, engaging, and accessible, particularly for children who might not have other exposure to the performing arts. That is something Glaze allowed him to do in Newry, Northern Ireland, until he could perfect his own technique. "We run in space, we carve in space, we play with level changes. I don't look for the perfect second or the perfect arabesque; it's what each of these young men and women can give me," he told *Dance Teacher Magazine*. "It's *their* arabesque. It's *their* second position."

Bottom: Peter Rombult, Neil Donohoe, Mimi Hewlett, Sean Murphy, and Richard Ortner

Kate Ladenheim and CRAWL

CRAWL, a multidisciplinary performance series, was launched in December 2014 in New York City. Funded in part by The Boston Conservatory Alumni Entrepreneurial Grant Program, the series was an offshoot of alumna **Kate Ladenheim**'s (B.F.A. '11, contemporary dance) contemporary dance company, The People Movers. CRAWL introduced a new model for neighborhood-based arts events, targeted at the millennial generation, and was tasked with engaging audiences both intellectually and physically.

The concept centers on audience members watching a performance created by an emerging choreographer, then "crawling" to a local restaurant for a chance to socialize and discuss the piece. Then, the audience returns to the original venue for a second performance, which segues into a third artistic act that utilizes music, visual arts, and/or film. Each CRAWL event concludes with a celebration, giving audiences and artists a chance to meet each other, discuss the work, and build relationships around their communal experience.

Committed to community involvement, CRAWL partners with local businesses, who help to promote performances and build audiences. CRAWL aims to shift the way millennials relate to art by reimagining the artistic experience and breaking down traditional barriers between audience members and performers. Ladenheim's artistic vision focuses on creating discourse around socially and culturally relevant topics and pushes audiences to think abstractly within the context of traditional performance.

Bottom left: Kate Ladenheim

Senior Dance Showing

In 2016, dance seniors **Ariane Michaud** and **Katharina Schier** (both B.F.A. '16, contemporary dance) spearheaded a new initiative to establish the Conservatory's first-ever senior showcase for dancers.

The showing, a performance intended to introduce and connect graduating students with industry professionals, was held at The Gibney Center in New York City on March 16, 2016 and featured more than fourteen Conservatory seniors, including: **Demetrius Burns**, **Jade Chauvin**, **Elijah Dillehay**, **Emily Jerant-Hendrickson**, **Cacia LaCount**, **Key'Aira Lockett**, **MacKenzie Mathis**, **Kelsey McCormack**, **Taylor Rodman**,

Ariane Michaud, **Katharina Schier**, and **Dorrie Silver**.

Schier and Michaud were inspired to take on the endeavor with the encouragement of **Cathy Young**, dean of dance. To make the event possible, Michaud and Schier worked with several of the Conservatory's departments to plan, produce, and market the event. They also organized several fundraising efforts, including a Kickstarter campaign and an on-campus bake sale.

"Working on this project has taught me many things specifically related to producing, creating, organizing, and marketing a show," Michaud reflected. "However, perhaps the most valuable lessons have been in learning what it takes to be a good collaborator and in developing a positive team-oriented working environment."

Because of Michaud and Schier's effort, the project enabled students to make meaningful connections with working industry professionals and Conservatory alumni in the New York City area. The Conservatory has since decided to formalize the program as an annual capstone course for seniors, which began in the fall of 2016.

Jonathon Heyward and Rachel Hedding

Jonathon Heyward received his bachelor of music in cello performance in 2014 from The Boston Conservatory and immediately garnered international attention after a career-launching win of the 2015 Young Conductors Competition.

Heyward bested 260 candidates and was announced as the first-prize winner of the 54th International Competition for Young Conductors at the Besançon Music Festival in France, the most prestigious conducting competition in the world. Only 23 years old, Heyward made history as one of the youngest entrants to win the competition.

Heyward enrolled at the Conservatory as a cello student of the revered cellist **Andrew Mark**. His interest in conducting—an artform that fascinated him since childhood—inspired him to supplement his cello training with studies in conducting, which he began in 2012 with conductor **Andrew Altenbach**, the Conservatory's music director for opera

studies. Heyward was assistant conductor for the school's Opera Department from 2012 to 2014, during which time he worked on several Conservatory productions, such as *La Bohème*, *die Zauberflöte*, and *The Rape of Lucretia*. In 2013, Heyward was named music director for the Conservatory's production of *Mooch the Messy*, a children's opera that toured multiple Boston-area schools and museums.

Upon graduation from the Conservatory, Heyward pursued a master of music in orchestral conducting at the Royal Academy of Music in London. **Sir Mark Elder**, the renowned music director of the Hallé Orchestra in Manchester, England, where Heyward served as assistant conductor, described Heyward as "a bright rising star of the conducting world." He added: "I am looking forward to watching his development in the variety of roles that offer a young conductor the most wonderful platform to develop the skills

and understanding needed to build an international career."

Heyward's success at the Conservatory was made possible by The Hank Hankinson Scholarship Fund, which was established by Boston Conservatory Overseer **Rachael Zammiello Hedding** (B.M. '65, voice) in honor of her deceased classmate and friend, **Herbert "Hank" Hankinson** (B.M. '65). Hankinson attended the Conservatory on a full scholarship and, after graduation, taught at Berklee College of Music for twenty-five years. He lived in Warren, Rhode Island and performed frequently as a professional musician throughout New England. Hankinson died in 2001 at the age of 64. The Conservatory awards the Hankinson scholarship to male African American music students from the Music Division who demonstrate significant academic growth, artistic discipline, and an emerging talent.

The Entrepreneurial Spirit

The evolution of Boston Conservatory has always been fueled by the entrepreneurial spirit of its students and faculty. While some artists wait for fortune to favor them, many artists waste no time in creating their own opportunities.

Taylor Ambrosio-Wood (B.M. '15, percussion), who studied under percussion and marimba faculty member **Nancy Zeltsman**, began taking private lessons in composition with noted composer **Marti Epstein**, who is on the faculty at both the Conservatory and Berklee College of Music. Ambrosio-Wood took advantage of the pre-merger ability to study with Epstein by crossregistering for classes at Berklee through the ProArts Consortium. It was then that Ambrosio-Wood began composing, with a focus on film and video game scoring. She was later accepted into the composition master's program at Berklee's Valencia, Spain campus, where, in 2016, she completed her first year.

Conservatory student **Sarah Brown** (B.F.A. '17, musical theater) made her way to the Berklee Internet Radio Network (BIRN) station just as the ink was drying on the merger agreement. A California native, Brown learned about the Berklee student-run station and applied to join—a fitting extracurricular activity, as she considered a career in broadcasting. After completing the training program, Brown got her own weekly show, *How to Pop*, broadcasting music that she was not sure the Berklee community would appreciate. "At first, I was intimidated to join because Berklee students have such distinct tastes in music," she said. "But I [wanted to share my] love of pop tunes and Top 40 radio."

Her show, however, was an immediate success, and the experience she has gained as a radio host has been invaluable.

"Enterprising" hardly describes the efforts of **Katsuya Yuasa** (M.M. '15, clarinet), who is constantly looking for ways to work with other artists and find new performance venues. Yuasa, who was a member of the Conservatory Connections program, was among the first to jump into collaborations with Berklee students, including his 2016 performance of Svante Henryson's *Off Pist* with Berklee cellist **Roman Soto**. Yuasa, who also works to find sponsorships for his public performances, said, "I like to create opportunities and find new places to perform. It is part of being a musician today."

Left: Taylor Ambrosio-Wood; *Center:* Sarah Brown; *Right:* Katsuya Yuasa

John Cage Performance at the Museum of Fine Arts

In January 2016, **Simon Dyer** (M.M. '16, G.P.D. '17, opera) curated a unique performance of John Cage's *Song Books* (*Solos for Voice 3–92)* at the Museum of Fine Arts, Boston in the Art of Asia Galleries as an independent venture.

Cage, who was inspired by the ancient Chinese divination text, the *I-Ching*, created a multitude of works over his career that were based on the concept of chance. In 1970, Cage completed the composition of his *Song Books*—a large collection of songs that each fall under one of four categories: song, theater, song with electronics, and theater with electronics.

The performers, **Rachel Barg** (B.M. '16, voice), **Lauren Cook** (M.M. '16, voice), **Simon Dyer** (M.M. '16, G.P.D. '17, opera), **Natalie Logan** (M.M. '16), **Andrew O'Shanick** (M.M. '16, opera), and **Tzytle Steinman** (B.M. '16, voice), explored the idea of chance, weaving together a visually and musically energetic environment.

Bolivian Chamber Music Society

Sergio Escalera (B.M. '14, piano) was awarded one of the Conservatory's first-ever student entrepreneurial grants in 2013 for his project, Sociedad Boliviana de Música de Cámara (SBMC), or the Bolivian Chamber Music Society. SBMC was the first organization in Bolivia specifically dedicated to offering high-caliber chamber music performances, as well as concerts, master classes, and coaching for musicians of all ages and levels. Escalera, along with two other musicians from Bolivia, was inspired to establish SBMC as a way to provide professional music education within the country, so that promising artists would not have to seek it elsewhere. The mission and vision for SBMC is to build a platform for Bolivian musicians to develop and share their art, ultimately enriching the community and larger region.

Boston Percussion Group

Boston Percussion Group (BPeG) is a contemporary ensemble/rock band whose dynamic performances challenge the definition of classical music through repertoire ranging from Steve Reich to Frank Zappa. BPeG's signature is adapting popular music not written for percussion instruments, as it allows casual listeners to connect with percussion instruments through familiar tunes.

Comprised of six percussion/marimba Conservatory alumni, **Jeremy Barnett** (M.M. '11), **Brian Calhoon** (M.M. '09), **Jonathan Hess** (M.M. '11), **Dane Palmer** (M.M. '13), **Matt Sharrock** (G.P.D. '13, M.M. '11), and **Greg Simonds** (G.P.D. '10), BPeG was the recipient of a Boston Conservatory Alumni Entrepreneurial Grant. With this funding, BPeG presented a five-school musical education tour to

public schools in Greater Boston in 2015, in addition to their standard performance season. Their work in the public schools taught students how to listen, identify different elements of music, and learn about the various percussion instruments.

The Video Game Orchestra
and the Videri String Quartet

In recent decades, the music underscoring video games has become as complex and sophisticated as the scores for film and television, and the video game music industry has boomed. Several innovative musicians who have studied at The Boston Conservatory have made it their mission to showcase this new genre.

Shota Nakama, who graduated with a master of music in guitar performance in 2011, started working with video game music while getting his undergraduate degree in film composition at Berklee College of Music. In 2008, he founded the Video Game Orchestra (VGO), an ensemble that combines rock, orchestral, and choral elements to reenvision video game scores into a new genre he dubs "rockestral." With VGO, he has orchestrated music for *Final Fantasy XV* and *Kingdom Hearts*.

Nakama told *STAGES* magazine in 2015 that he prides himself on his ability to network and build relationships. He and his collaborators, many of whom

also graduated from Berklee or the Conservatory, have created wildly popular music experiences at venues like Boston's Symphony Hall and Seattle's Paramount Theater. They took a four-city tour of China, the highlight of which was a sell-out crowd at a 3,000-seat venue in Taiwan.

The VGO's work appeals to a broad audience. "Our audience consists of all kinds of people because our concerts integrate the musicality of orchestral concerts with rock show entertainment," he says. "They are always energetic and passionate—we have people screaming and expressing their excitement."

Another group embracing video game music is the Videri String Quartet, three members of which studied at the Conservatory: **Lizzie Jones** (G.P.D. '18, violin), **Roselie Samter** (M.M. '09, viola), and **Jeremiah-Everard Barcus** (M.M. '09, viola). The fourth member, violinist **Michael Hustedde**, graduated from Boston University.

Founded in 2012, the Videri String Quartet is committed to reinventing the string quartet experience for the modern listener. The quartet utilizes a unique hybrid of aural and visual narratives, often performing standard quartet repertoire such as Haydn, or Janáček, alongside music from video games, such as *Halo* and *BioShock*. The quartet has been featured on video game soundtracks for *The Magic Circle*, *Beat Sports*, and *Neocolonialism*.

For Videri's members, video game music is as much about bringing their training to a new area of music as it is about reaching new audiences. According to the Quartet's website, "Videri seeks to explore the ways in which video game music impacts its listeners, discover the parallels between traditional classical music and video game music, celebrate the dynamic link between music and storytelling, and to use video game music as a means of expression for children and young adults."

Top left: The Video Game Orchestra; *Right:* Shota Nakama; *Below:* Videri String Quartet members Michael Hustedde, Lizzie Jones, Roselie Samter, and Jeremiah-Everard Barcus

Timeline of Events

Boston Conservatory of Music,

MASON & HAMLIN'S NEW MARBLE BUILDING,

154 TREMONT STREET.

OPENING OF FALL TERM, MONDAY, SEPTEMBER 16, 1867.

DIRECTOR, - - - - - MR. JULIUS EICHBERG.

REFERENCES:

His Excellency A. H. BULLOCK,   Surg. Gen. WM. J. DALE,
Hon. JOHN A. ANDREW,   HOWARD M. TICKNOR,
Col. HENRY WARE,   CHARLES F. SHIMMIN,
Col. THOMAS E. CHICKERING,   LORING B. BARNES,
JOHN S. DWIGHT,   OLIVER DITSON,
Dr. J. BAXTER UPHAM,   HENRY MASON,
THERON J. DALE,   FRANCIS H. UNDERWOOD,
AUGUSTUS FLAGG,   Dr. JOHN P. ORDWAY.

BOARD OF INSTRUCTION:

Messrs. JULIUS EICHBERG,   Messrs. J. B SHARLAND,
         AUGUST KREISSMANN,   SOLON WILDER,
         HUGO LEONHARD,   AUGUST SUCK,
         EUGENE THAYER,   J. RAMETTI,
         HOWARD M. DOW,   M. ARBUCKLE.

☞ Not more than from three to four pupils in one class.

Signor J. B. TORRICELLI, Professor of Italian Language.
Prof. MOSES T. BROWN, Teacher of Elocution and Vocal Culture.

The above Institution is now ready to receive pupils desirous of obtaining a THOROUGH MUSICAL EDUCATION at the SMALLEST POSSIBLE EXPENSE.

It will be seen, by an attentive examination of the following statement, that the Boston Conservatory of Music essentially differs in its plan from other musical institutions in this country, combining, as it does, the most commendable features of European Conservatories with such improvements as were suggested by the Director's long experience in Europe and America.

1860s

May 1865: The United States' four-year Civil War ends.

1866: Julius Eichberg, violinist, composer, and teacher, begins discussions with Boston's music community about establishing a "conservatory of music" in the city. Advertisements appear in newspapers seeking instructors and alerting students that the school is being organized.

February 11, 1867: Julius Eichberg opens the Boston Conservatory of Music at 154 Tremont Street, across from Boston Common, in a fourth-floor studio, where he had previously run a violin school. The New England Conservatory of Music opens one week later, founded by Eben Tourjée.

1867: As would be the case throughout much of the Conservatory's history, there is some confusion over the school's name, as it conflicts with other organizations of the same name. The Boston Conservatory, a renowned museum of specimen plants, had burned to the ground in an overnight fire a few years prior to the opening of Julius Eichberg's music school. Also, there is a Boston Conservatory of Music located in the Midwest, which closes prior to Eichberg's filing of the school's formal incorporation papers.

January 1868: Advertisements in Boston's newspapers tout the school's faculty and the types of instruction offered: "musical instruments, solfeggio, harmony, singing, chorus-singing, piano, organ, violin, violoncello, bass, flute, cornet … and other orchestral instruments."

1870s

1870: The first diploma from the Boston Conservatory of Music is issued to Richard E. Bobbitt, who successfully completed a multiyear program that included instruction in harmony and theory.

February 4, 1873: Julius Eichberg's operetta *The Doctor of Alcantara* is performed in Washington, D.C. by the first African American opera company in the United States. The news of the historic night is announced on the front page of *The New York Times*.

1876: Julius Eichberg and his brother, Isidor Eichberg, organize the Conservatory as a corporation.

February 6, 1877: The oldest recovered review of a Conservatory performance appears in print. "The pupils' matinee by the scholars of The Boston Conservatory of Music occurred at Tremont Temple … under the direction of Mr. Julius Eichberg," *The Boston Globe* reported. Among those who performed are: Albert Van Raalte (violin instructor) and Lillie P. Richards, Marie Murdoch, Lillian Chandler, Lillian Shattuck, and Frank Litchheld (students).

1877: *Dwight's Journal of Music* writes of the Conservatory: "Surely there can be no doubt of its being the best violin school in the country."

1878: Julius Eichberg recruits top Conservatory students to form the Eichberg Quartet, the first known all-female, professional string quartet. By 1884 it is touring nationally and internationally. The most famous iteration is comprised of Lillian Shattuck and Lettie Launder (violin), Emma Grebe (viola), and Laura Webster (cello).

1880s

1880s: According to media accounts at the time, acclaimed concert violinist Joseph Douglass—grandson of noted abolitionist Frederick Douglass—received his classical training at both New England Conservatory of Music and Boston Conservatory of Music. Douglass is one of the first African American performers to garner national and international renown.

1881: The Conservatory is teaching 1,000 pupils per year, including grade school–aged children. In his book *The Memorial History of Boston* (1881), John S. Dwight writes of Julius Eichberg's school as having immediate success. "In one department, the Violin School, it is unique. Here Mr. Eichberg has accomplished wonders," Dwight wrote of the students, some as young as 8 years old.

1881: The Boston Symphony Orchestra is founded.

1886: *Grove Music Encyclopedia* reports that the Conservatory has become one of the leading music schools in the country, having educated some 15,000 pupils.

May 22, 1887: Cornet prodigy Perry George "P.G." Lowery, believed to be the first African American student to graduate from the Conservatory, arrives in Boston from Kansas for instruction with Henry C. Brown. (Julius Eichberg had offered Lowery a scholarship after reading about his prowess on the cornet.) Lowery's stepbrother, trombonist Ed Greene, travels with Lowery and also studies music in Boston.

1890s

June 20, 1890: The Conservatory is thrust into the limelight after a report in *The Boston Daily Globe* recounts the story of Etta N. Jewett, a Conservatory music student who went missing. The paper reports that the student "went on a lark" and was "taken into custody" in Albany, New York "at the request of her friends." Jewett, who was en route from Boston to her home in Indiana, was described in the report as "an extremely pretty brunette of pleasing manners and vivacious temperament." She was picked up after a clergyman there received a letter from a Conservatory instructor who was worried that Jewett—whom he described as "headstrong" with "a love of fun"—was travelling alone and "enjoying a round of gayety" in Albany. Jewett was not charged; she was only detained until her family could retrieve her.

January 20, 1893: Boston Conservatory of Music founder Julius Eichberg dies unexpectedly at the age of 68 from pneumonia at his home on Marlborough Street in the Back Bay neighborhood of Boston. In his obituary, *The New York Times* called Eichberg "one of the greatest violin teachers in this country." In the twenty-six years that Eichberg ran the Conservatory, he expanded course offerings while keeping the class sizes small, created opportunities for women and minorities, and was a leader in Boston's classical music scene. After his death, management of the school is assumed by Eichberg's brother, Isidor Eichberg.

December 1894: Isidor Eichberg, Julius's brother, dies. The Eichberg family—Julius's widow, Sophie, and their daughter, Annie—transfers ownership of the school to local business owner R. Marriner Floyd.

Julius Eichberg

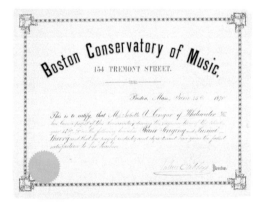

1870: The first diploma

Lillian Shattuck, left

197

DEDICATED TO
P. G. LOWERY
WORLD'S CHALLENGING COLORED
CORNETIST AND BAND MASTER

250 Huntington Avenue

June 19, 1896: Boston Conservatory of Music is incorporated under Massachusetts Law and announces a new management team in local newspapers. R. Marriner Floyd—who ran a musical instrument and jewelry-making company on the same floor as the Conservatory—takes over operation of the school. Herman P. Chelius, who was hired by Eichberg to teach organ and piano, assumes the role of music director for the school.

January 29, 1898: A "serious" fire of unknown origin rips through the fourth floor of 154 and 155 Tremont Street, in a section of the building that houses both the Conservatory and director R. Marriner Floyd's jewelry offices, according to newspaper reports. The fire causes an estimated $10,000 in damage, about $2,000 of which was damage to the building.

1900s

1901: Conservatory faculty members give the first concert performed at the school's new home in the Odd Fellows building on Tremont Street. The event is hosted by the school's director, R. Marriner Floyd. Performers include Frank La Raine Chamberlain, Gertrude C. Soule, and Winetta Lamson.

June 27, 1901: An involuntary petition of bank-ruptcy is filed against the Boston Conservatory of Music, according to *The New York Times*. The creditors listed are: The Oliver Ditson Company, a music publishing company, which is owed $4,545; J. Montgomery Sears, the landlord of the Conservatory's original home at 154 Tremont Street, with a claim of $281.42; and the Conservatory's music director Herman P. Chelius, who claims he is owed $4,920.

1902: In a dispatch picked up by newspapers everywhere, Perry George "P.G." Lowery writes to his family that he owes a great deal of his success to his teacher Henry C. Brown and the so-called Boston Cornet—made by the Boston Musical Instrument Company—that Brown gifted to Lowery upon completion of his studies at the Conservatory.

1905: Official incorporation papers reorganizing the Conservatory for a third time are signed and filed by R. Marriner Floyd and others.

1910s

1910–1914: Little is known about the school or how many courses are offered during this time, although it is listed on the state's roster of businesses.

August 15, 1914: Boston Conservatory of Music is reestablished as The Boston Conservatory and College of Oratory and lists R. Marriner Floyd as president.

1915: Sophie Eichberg, widow of Julius Eichberg, dies in London, where she lives with their daughter, Annie Eichberg King Lane.

1917: Renowned opera conductor Agide Jacchia is named conductor of the Boston Pops Orchestra.

1917–1919: Confusion over the school's name continues. Classes are offered in listings by the Boston Conservatory of Music, but also listed on flyers as College of Oratory, although there is no published catalog for this period.

1920s

1920: R. Marriner Floyd dies and his estate is liquidated. Boston Pops conductor Agide Jacchia assumes control of The Boston Conservatory and College of Oratory and immediately works to reinvigorate the school.

February 2, 1920: Agide Jacchia reorganizes the school together with Frank Leveroni, Walter E. Hammett, John Dixwell, and Samuel L. Bailen.

1920: Agide Jacchia establishes a Grand Opera Department at the Conservatory, which is something he found to be lacking in United States music schools. He hires his wife, Ester Ferrabini Jacchia, a critically acclaimed singer best known for her portrayal of the title role in *Carmen*, to the opera faculty.

1920: Albert Alphin begins studies as a student at the Conservatory. A short time later, Iride Pilla enrolls and begins studying opera with Ester Ferrabini Jacchia. Both Alphin and Pilla go on to teach at the school years later.

1924: Albert Alphin is appointed to the faculty.

1925: Facing economic difficulty, Agide Jacchia tries unsuccessfully to obtain financial support for the Conservatory from the City of Boston. Jacchia returns to Eichberg's model of offering free instruction and scholarships to students who show musical talent but cannot afford tuition.

1927: Albert Alphin resigns from his teaching position at the Conservatory to start his National Associated Studios of Music, which provides private music teachers to programs in the region and New York City.

1928: Agide Jacchia becomes ill and begins a period of travel to search for a cure. He continues to run the school through mail and telegraph messages. He and his family make several return trips to Boston over the next few years.

1928: The Boston Conservatory and College of Oratory moves to a new location at 256 Huntington Avenue, opposite Symphony Hall.

1928–1930: Albert Alphin produces radio programs in recital halls throughout the city and holds chamber recitals in the restaurant downstairs from the Conservatory.

1930s

November 29, 1932: Agide Jacchia dies in Italy.

1932–1933: Ester Ferrabini Jacchia oversees the Conservatory from Italy in coordination with Albert Alphin in the United States, who runs the school's day-to-day operations from his business next door.

July 1933: The family of Agide Jacchia transfers ownership of the Conservatory to Albert Alphin, who begins a hiring wave that includes a number of instructors that he worked with at the National Associated Studios of Music.

August 24, 1934: Hans Ebell, a renowned teacher on whom Alphin built his newly revamped Conservatory, dies in what police initially believe is a murder plot that involves Ebell's ex-wife and her new boyfriend. Stories of the investigation appear in New England newspapers for years, but no charges were ever filed against Ebell's ex-wife. In an interesting

twist, Ebell's signature continues to appear on Conservatory diplomas for a few years after his death.

December 13, 1935: The institution's name is changed back to Boston Conservatory of Music.

1936: Boston Conservatory of Music dissolves as a business corporation and becomes a nonprofit organization under Alphin's leadership.

July 1936: The Conservatory purchases 26 Fenway.

September 1936: Classes are held for the first time at 26 Fenway.

August 1937: *The Boston Globe* reports that when the Conservatory opens on September 13, two staff members will be added to the faculty for the fall term: Caroline Hudson-Alexander, distinguished soprano and teacher, and pianist George Fior.

April 21, 1938: Boston Conservatory of Music receives authorization from the state to grant bachelor of music degrees. Later in the year, the Conservatory becomes fully accredited.

September 1939: 32 Fenway is acquired. The school begins its move to the Fenway strip from Huntington Avenue.

1940s

1940: William Andrew Rhodes is awarded a composition degree and is the first African American composer to graduate from a Boston institution.

1940–1943: The Conservatory purchases several buildings to be used as dormitories, including 24 Fenway, 40 Fenway, and 54 Fenway.

1941: Albert Alphin changes his title from manager to director of the Boston Conservatory of Music.

1943: Jan Veen establishes The Boston Conservatory Dance Division. It is the first complete department of dance at the college level in the country, according to music historian Andrea Olmstead.

1920: Ester Ferrabini Jacchia

1940: William Andrew Rhodes

1943: Jan Veen formalizes the dance department

1946: Harlan F. Grant

1948: Construction of 31 Hemenway

Master of Music Degree at Boston Conservatory

The Boston Conservatory of Music, Albert Alphin, director, has been given authority by the Board of Collegiate Authority of the Commonwealth of Massachusetts to grant the degree, Master of Music. Programs of study for this degree in the fields of applied music, composition and music education will be offered at the beginning of the Fall term.

1957: Masters degrees authorized

March 28, 1943: The Conservatory receives a notable review by *The Boston Globe*'s music critic: "One of the most enjoyable chamber music concerts of the season was given at the Boston Conservatory yesterday." The article describes a performance by the Boston Conservatory String Quartet, "whose members (all Boston Symphony men) are Gaston Elcus and Norbert Lauga, violins; Jean LeFranc, viola; Jacobus Langendoen, cello. Georg Fior, pianist, assisted."

1943–1946: Two parcels of land are purchased on Hemenway Street for a new building project.

August 15, 1944: Albert Alphin marries Conservatory alumna Katherine M. Shepherd, who serves as a house mother in the dorms along the Fenway.

1945: World War II ends and the Conservatory enrolls a number of new students studying on the G.I. Bill, which prompts Alphin's second hiring spree.

1945: Schillinger House, later called Berklee School of Music, is founded by Lawrence Berk.

1946: Harlan F. Grant founds the Drama Department.

1948: Albert Alphin starts construction on the school's 31 Hemenway Street building, a project that had been delayed because of a materials shortage during World War II. Alphin envisions a state-of-the-art auditorium and recital space so that the buildings along the Fenway strip can be used as dormitories.

June 4, 1948: Reverend Arthur B. Whitney, president of the Conservatory's Board of Trustees, confers degrees and certificates to the graduating class at a ceremony held at New England Mutual Hall, 225 Clarendon Street.

April 17, 1949: Students, faculty, and guest artists perform a full program to mark the official opening of 31 Hemenway Street. The concert is held in the building's auditorium (later known as the mainstage, or Boston Conservatory Theater).

June 10, 1949: The first commencement held in the auditorium of 31 Hemenway features The Conservatory Chorus, led by Grover J. Oberle, and The Conservatory Orchestra, conducted by Alan Hovhaness. The speaker is David J. Holden, associate professor of music at Mount Holyoke

College. Degrees are awarded to students who have come from as far away as Laguna Beach, California. Two Conservatory certificates in piano are given to Fei Hsu and Sze Chia Wei, both from Shanghai, China.

1950s

January 29, 1950: The Boston Conservatory String Quartet, comprised of faculty members Gaston Elcus, Harry Dickson, Albert Bernard, and Jacobus Langendoen, give a concert of Mozart's Piano Quartet No. 1 and Handel's Sonata in G minor in the Conservatory's auditorium at 31 Hemenway Street. Pianist Lee Wei-Ning, who teaches harmony, counterpoint, and theory at the Conservatory, performs with the group.

June 4, 1950: A concert featuring original works by composition students is performed by Conservatory students and is held in the auditorium at 31 Hemenway Street. Composers include: Stephen Lestina, Lawrence Bardouille, and George Grice, who later makes a name for himself in the world of jazz as Gigi Gryce.

February 8, 1951: Boston Conservatory of Music is authorized to award Bachelor of Fine Arts degrees in drama and dance.

1951: Dance Department founder Jan Veen hosts a series of student recitals featuring original choreography. Among those participating are: Wallace James; Jack Splaine; Carl Fauci; Martha Royce; and Francis Boyd Ryland, who continues to support the Conservatory as of 2017. The program from one of the recitals notes that Splaine, Fauci, Ryland, and Al Bosbach had served in the United States Armed Forces.

May 28, 1955: The Boston Conservatory Opera Workshop, under the direction of Iride Pilla, presents scenes and excerpts in the Conservatory's auditorium at 31 Hemenway Street.

March 17, 1956: The Conservatory's Theater Department gives the first of two performances of Arthur Miller's three-act drama *The Crucible*, directed by department head Harlan F. Grant.

June 8, 1956: Reverend Dr. Bradford Gale, the pastor of the First Parish Church of Salem, Massachusetts, delivers the commencement address at the ceremony held in the

Conservatory's auditorium at 31 Hemenway Street. A baccalaureate service was held earlier in the day with the Reverend Henry B. Whitney, pastor of the Peabody Unitarian Church, giving the sermon.

February 11, 1957: Authorization is granted by the Massachusetts state legislature for the Conservatory to award Master of Music and Master of Music Education degrees.

May 11, 1957: Conservatory students stage a benefit production of the musical *Finian's Rainbow* to raise money for a group of Hungarian students to attend the Conservatory. The Hungarian students were identified by Darcy Wilson, chairman of New England CARE, while he was in Hungary following the 1956 revolution. The five performances were supported by some of Boston's leading citizens.

1960s

October 1960: Faculty members, including Grace Hunter, Attilio Poto, Robert Dumm, Serge Conus, Gordon and Betsy Argo, Robert Petite, Rouben Gregorian, Philine Falco, Iride Pilla, Ruth Ambrose, Robert Gilman, and Jan Veen organize a series of Tuesday evening concerts that are presented in the Concert Room at 26 Fenway.

June 9, 1961: The Conservatory holds its commencement ceremony in the auditorium of 31 Hemenway Street. "The program features the Conservatory chorus and orchestra under the direction of Rouben Gregorian," according to *The Boston Globe*. Max Kaplan, director of The Arts Center at Boston University, also gives a talk entitled "Music in a Technological Age."

September 16, 1963: Fall registration is announced in Boston newspapers and promises robust offerings for degree programs. Evening instruction in music, drama, and dance will be available for those unable to attend classes during the day.

June 4, 1965: Robert Dumm, a faculty member from 1958 to 1968, who served as the Conservatory's dean when he was 25 years old, leaves on a 25-city tour in which he conducts piano workshops for teachers and students.

June 12, 1965: Robert A. Choate, former dean of Boston University School of Fine Arts, gives the address at the Conservatory's graduation ceremony, which is held in the Conservatory's auditorium at 31 Hemenway Street.

1965: 54 Fenway and 8 Fenway buildings are purchased.

1966: The Conservatory's yearbook, *Apollo*, publishes an unsigned history of the Conservatory, which marks the first known attempt at recording the school's past.

1967: Conservatory Director Albert Alphin uses the occasion of the school's centennial to announce his retirement and announces George A. Brambilla as his replacement. At the time of this leadership change, the Conservatory has 1,100 students, 500 of whom are enrolled full time. Alphin goes on to serve at the school's treasurer and is a regular presence on campus.

1967: William A. Seymour joins the faculty and later serves as dean.

February 11, 1967: To mark the Conservatory's one hundredth anniversary, the school hosts a concert featuring students and faculty performing with the Conservatory Orchestra under the direction of Rouben Gregorian. News accounts of the celebration note that not even the snowstorm that blanketed the city the night before could stop the festivities.

May 1967: A gala centennial dinner is held at the Sheraton Plaza Hotel in the Back Bay.

June 1, 1968: The Conservatory awards degrees to fifty-seven students at a commencement ceremony held in the school's auditorium, featuring a concert by the Conservatory orchestra and chorus, with Rouben Gregorian conducting. The students also perform a contemporary work by faculty member Avram David.

1970s

July 25, 1970: Diana Dohrmann, a piano student at the Conservatory, wins the Miss Massachusetts title and goes on to represent the state in the Miss America pageant in Atlantic City.

1960: Attilio Poto conducts Tuesday evening concerts

1965: 8 Fenway building purchased

1967: William Seymour joins the faculty

1973: Opera department reorganized

1973: Dance troupe trip to Portugal

1980: Rouben Gregorian retires

December 1971: Rouben Gregorian conducts the Conservatory's orchestra in a concert of Christmas music that is broadcast on live television by WCVB, Boston's Channel 5.

1972: Composer John Clement Adams joins the faculty and continues to teach until 2000.

September 1972: A full slate of free classical recitals featuring both students and faculty is announced for the school year.

1973: President George A. Brambilla reorganizes the Opera Department. Run by John Moriarty, the opera program is combined for a time with the New England Conservatory of Music to take better advantage of the resources at both schools.

June 23, 1973: The Conservatory's dance troupe leaves Boston for a five-week stay as the resident company at the International Academy of Dance in Portugal. The troupe had been founded by Jan Veen. James Bynum organizes this and previous trips of the school's dancers to Portugal and Switzerland.

September 12, 1973: Albert Alphin dies.

January 22, 1976: John Moriarty directs and conducts a program of three one-act operas in the Conservatory's theater at 31 Hemenway Street. The program premieres Pasatlieri's *Signor Deluso*, Barber's *Hand of Bridge*, and Bernstein's *Trouble in Tahiti*.

June 1977: At the end of the school year, Drama Department founder Harlan F. Grant and his wife, Florence, retire. Harlan began teaching at the Conservatory in 1933 and taught theater arts, art history, and drama, and Florence taught stage makeup since 1950.

1979: The Board of Trustees replaces President George A. Brambilla with Dale A. DuVall, marking the beginning of the Conservatory's most unstable period in recent history.

1980s

1980: Rouben Gregorian, who joined the faculty in 1953, retires. During his tenure, Gregorian taught violin and composition, and led the string ensemble.

1980: The Conservatory undergoes an accreditation process that unearths problems with the school's financial stability and leadership structure.

1980: The City of Boston cites the Conservatory for dozens of building code violations in its five dormitories along the Fenway.

1981: With the school's accreditation at risk, trustees tap former dean William A. Seymour to lead the school's faculty, staff, and students through the changes needed to retain its ranking. The staff effort is successful, and the board dismisses Dale A. DuVall and offers Seymour the presidency.

1981: William A. Seymour begins his tenure as president of the Conservatory.

1982: The school's name is officially changed to The Boston Conservatory.

May 15, 1982: John Williams, noted composer and conductor of the Boston Pops, delivers an improvised commencement address to the Conservatory's seventy-three graduating members in a ceremony at the Conservatory theater. Williams speaks briefly about his own career and about the joys of the performing arts. He tells the audience that some of the highest quality of musical training and performance in the world is taking place in America, *The Boston Globe* reports. Williams is given an honorary doctor of music degree.

May 14, 1983: Marge Champion, author, actress, dancer, and choreographer, is given an honorary doctor of fine arts degree at the Conservatory's commencement ceremony, held in the Old South Church. Ninety-one candidates receive master of music, bachelor of music, and bachelor of fine arts degrees. Two of the graduates receive awards for academic achievement.

May 1984: At the commencement ceremony, held at the Museum of Fine Arts, seven master of music degrees are granted, including one in composition to Maryam Aline Moshaver of Tehran, Iran. Forty students receive bachelor degrees in fine arts and in music.

May 11, 1985: At the commencement ceremony held in the Remis Auditorium of the Museum of

Fine Arts, Edward Villella, a former soloist with the New York City Ballet Company, receives an honorary doctor of humane letters "in recognition of his complete dedication to and relentless promotion of dance and the arts in America."

June 1985: *A History of The Boston Conservatory of Music* by Andrea Olmstead, then chair of the Music History Department, is published.

April 1986: With student enrollment up to 400, the Conservatory looks to expand beyond its 7 buildings on the Fenway and makes an unsuccessful bid to buy a former Catholic school in Jamaica Plain.

May 9, 1987: More than seventy graduates are given bachelor's and master's degrees in music, theater, and dance at graduation ceremonies held in the Remis Auditorium of the Museum of Fine Arts. Harry Ellis Dickson, associate conductor of the Boston Pops Orchestra and violinist in the Boston Symphony Orchestra, addresses the graduates. The ceremony marks the Conservatory's 120th year. Dickson is presented with an honorary doctor of music degree by President William A. Seymour.

June 1988: The Conservatory bestows an honorary degree on Alice Tully, a trained opera singer-turned-arts patron and philanthropist, who addresses the graduating class.

1988: The Boston Conservatory Student Government Association is formed.

1988: The Housing and Student Services Office, including room assignment and billing, are reorganized.

May 7, 1989: The Conservatory awards degrees to fifty-nine students during commencement ceremonies at the Museum of Fine Arts, its neighbor on the Fenway. During the ceremony an honorary degree is presented to Broadway composer Harry Kreiger.

1989: The dean of students position is established.

1989–1990 academic year: A number of new student-run clubs are launched.

1990s

1990: The Conservatory's Student Government President becomes a member of the school's President's Cabinet.

June 1990: The Conservatory awards an honorary degree to 90-year-old Jester Hairston, an actor, composer, conductor, and leading expert on African American spirituals and gospel music.

1991: The premiere issue of the student newspaper, later known as *The Marquee,* is printed.

1991: Family and Friends Weekend launches as part of the Conservatory's year-long 125th anniversary celebration.

February 11, 1992: The Conservatory celebrates its 125th anniversary. Among the events planned are a lecture series, concerts, and visiting guest artists.

March 8, 1992: The Conservatory hosts a special anniversary concert at Symphony Hall called "Point Me Towards Tomorrow: An Artist's Journey," with Marvin Hamlisch as the special guest. The concert was conceived and directed by Neil Donohoe and conducted by Ronald Feldman, with music produced, coordinated, and directed by faculty member Cathy Rand. The show features performances by students, faculty, alumni, and staff.

May 16, 1993: The Conservatory holds graduation for seventy-one graduates. Degrees awarded include five Conservatory diplomas, forty-one bachelor of arts, eight graduate performance certificates and artists' diplomas, and seventeen master of arts. An honorary degree is presented to William Warfield, concert bass-baritone singer and actor, who delivers the commencement address.

1993: The Boston Conservatory Student Union is established and features a snack bar called Rhythms, which was named by students. The Counterpoint Café later opens and replaces Rhythms in the 1995–1996 academic year.

1987: Harry Ellis Dickson given honorary doctor of music degree

1992: 125th anniversary celebration

1993: Rhythms snack bar opens

The Boston Conservatory

DANCE GALA

Honoring
Ruth S. Ambrose

1991: Ruth Sandholm Ambrose honored

1999: Richard Ortner hired

2003: Doriot Anthony Dwyer honored

June 1994: Carmen de Lavallade, actor-dancer-choreographer, gives the commencement address and is awarded an honorary degree.

June 1995: The Conservatory recognizes lyricist and playwright Adolph Green with an honorary degree at its graduation, which is the first to feature a student speaker from the senior class.

1996: *Illusions*, the Conservatory's literary magazine at the time, prints its first edition.

May 1997: Famed ballerina Violette Verdy speaks at commencement, where both she and Ruth Sandholm Ambrose are given honorary doctorate degrees. (Verdy was the former artistic director of the Boston Ballet and Paris Opera Ballet, and Ambrose was the artistic director emerita of the Conservatory's Dance Division.)

June 1997: William A. Seymour announces his retirement from the Conservatory.

June 1998: At William A. Seymour's last commencement as Conservatory president, he presents Broadway and television star Betty Buckley with an honorary degree after she addresses the graduates. The Distinguished Alumni Award is given to Diana Dohrmann (B.M. '71, music).

July 1998: Richard Ortner becomes the Conservatory's eighth president.

1999: Conservatory Connections, the school's community outreach program, is established by students. By 2016, the program provides 130 performances to more than forty community partners annually.

June 1999: Former President William A. Seymour returns to the Conservatory to receive an honorary degree and give the address to the graduating class.

1999–2000 academic year: The Conservatory undergoes its periodic accreditation check and the accreditation team cites the Conservatory's Student Affairs program as a "model for small colleges."

2000s

June 2000: The Conservatory gives an honorary degree to Trude Rittmann, a German Jewish composer who worked with George Balanchine and was later musical director for Aaron Copland and Leonard Bernstein.

June 2001: Meredith Monk, whose illustrious career includes credits as a composer, performer, director, vocalist, filmmaker, and composer, is given an honorary degree at the graduation ceremony.

2001–2002 school year: A musical theater ensemble is established for what was then called the Conservatory's Community Outreach program.

2002: Umoja, a club for African American students, and Spectrum, a club for students who are gay, lesbian, bisexual, or transgender, are formed.

June 2002: The Conservatory gives honorary degrees to American composer John Kander and musical theater lyricist Fred Ebb. The Distinguished Alumni Award is given to both Diane Arvanites (B.F.A. '80, dance) and Harriet Lundberg (M.M. '69, piano) at the commencement ceremony.

June 2003: The Conservatory gives an honorary degree to Doriot Anthony Dwyer, flute faculty member and first female principal chair of a major orchestra. The Distinguished Alumni Award is given to Doris Alberta (B.M. '63, music) at the commencement ceremony.

October 10, 2003: *The Boston Globe*'s Richard Dyer reports that baritone Sanford Sylvan has accepted the position of director of the Opera Department at the Conservatory, effective the following school year. "Sylvan joins another recent appointee, collaborative pianist Patty Thom, who was named chair of opera," the article states. "Sylvan began teaching part time at the [C]onservatory last year." In a statement, Karl Paulnack, then director of the Music Division, described Sylvan's master classes as "combining opera and musical theater, showing students that one discipline has much to teach the other."

May 15, 2004: The Conservatory awards 136 diplomas and certificates at the graduation ceremony, where honorary degrees are given to pianist Leon Fleisher and choreographer Murray Louis, a guest artist at the school. The Distinguished Alumni Award is given to Michelle Chassé (B.F.A. '92, dance).

September 2004: Music Division Director Karl Paulnack gives a powerful speech to the parents of the incoming freshman class on the importance of music. His words become an overnight sensation and attract the attention of scholars and celebrities alike. Since it was published on the Conservatory website in 2004, the speech has been requoted and referenced countless times, having been translated into at least 6 languages and appearing on more than 100,000 websites worldwide. With Paulnack's permission, performer Linda Ronstadt read a passage from his speech during her official testimony to the United States Congress on behalf of funding for the arts on March 31, 2009.

June 2005: The commencement ceremony recognizes the career of former opera faculty member Elisabeth Phinney, and the Distinguished Alumni Award is given to Frau Phinney's former student Victoria Livengood (M.M. '85, voice), who was also a Conservatory Overseer at the time.

2005: The Conservatory signs a contract with Northeastern University for dining services and for use of the Marino Center, a fitness and recreation center. Other fitness services begin.

2006: Board Trustee Mimi Hewlett leads the purchase of a parking lot on Hemenway Street, paving the way for the Hemenway Project.

2006: The Conservatory launches the Hemenway Project, the school's first-ever capital campaign, to raise funds for renovation and expansion of its 31 Hemenway Street building. The $30 million project allows for the addition of 16,000 square feet of rehearsal and studio performance space, renovations to the building's dance studios and office space, and improvements to the mainstage theater, including an expanded stage, a designated pit orchestra area, accessibility accommodations, improved seating, technical upgrades, and air conditioning.

June 2006: The Conservatory gives an honorary degree to dancer and choreographer Yuriko, known for her work with Martha Graham Dance Company. The Distinguished Alumni Award is given to James May (B.F.A. '85, dance).

2006: The Conservatory's Student Affairs Board of Trustees Committee is formed.

June 2007: Actor William Russell, known for his performances at Royal Shakespeare Company, National Theatre, and the Globe Theatre in England, receives an honorary degree at the commencement ceremony. The Distinguished Alumni Award is given to *Forbidden Broadway* creator Gerard Alessandrini (B.F.A. '77, musical theater).

2007: A Yoga Study program with the Kripalu Center is added to the school's wellness program offerings.

October 2007: *The Boston Globe* publishes a series of articles written by Linda Matchan that follow Conservatory student Stephanie Umoh as she trains with a hope to make the leap to Broadway. Umoh goes on to star in Broadway's 2009 revival of *Ragtime*.

2008: A music series at Brigham and Women's Hospital begins through Conservatory Connections.

June 2008: The Conservatory gives an honorary degree to Broadway director, choreographer, and performer Susan Stroman. The Distinguished Alumni Award is given to James Orleans (B.M. '81, music).

June 2009: Broadway legends Mary Rodgers and Barbara Cook are honored during the commencement ceremonies. The Distinguished Alumni Award is given to G. Clayton Taliaferro (G.P.D. '64, dance).

2009: The Conservatory establishes a partnership with Boston Cares, a nonprofit that organizes community volunteer projects.

2009: The Troubadours, comprised of opera and voice students, is formed for the Conservatory Connections program.

2009: Yoga for Musicians is first offered as a class for credit.

2007: Stephanie Umoh profiled

2006: Trustee Mimi Hewlett leads the Hemenway Project

2009: Barbara Cook honored at commencement ceremony

2010s

2011: Tokunaga retires

2012: 132 Ipswich project announced

2015: Exploration of merger with Berklee announced

June 2010: The Conservatory gives honorary degrees to theater producer Emanuel "Manny" Azenberg and Bruce Marks, a former ballet dancer who served as artistic director of the Boston Ballet. The Distinguished Alumni Award is given to Pam (Klappas) Pariseau (B.F.A. '88, musical theater).

2010: Alexander Technique and extracurricular yoga are first offered on campus.

October 2010: The renovated and expanded Boston Conservatory Theater at 31 Hemenway Street opens with celebratory grand opening performances featuring students and special guests, ten-time Tony Award–winner Tommy Tune, Joseph Silverstein, and alumnus Chad Kimball (B.F.A. '99, musical theater) from Broadway's *Memphis*.

2010: The Conservatory signs an agreement with Boston Children's Hospital's Sports Medicine group to establish on-campus hours.

2011: The tenth anniversary of the Conservatory's Drag Show is recognized.

2011: Conservatory promotional materials note that the school has more than 700 students, representing most of the United States and some 30 other countries.

2011: The grandchildren of former Conservatory director Agide Jacchia and his wife, opera faculty member Ester Ferrabini Jacchia, visit the Conservatory. Cristina Wax Zanobini and her brother Sergio Wax tour the school with President Richard Ortner and Eileen M. Meny, then director of development. The Jacchia family later names a seat in the renovated theater: "In Memory of Maestro A. Jacchia & Elsa Wax Jacchia."

June 2011: The Conservatory awards honorary degrees to Broadway performer and choreographer Tommy Tune and Tony Award–winning director Diane Paulus, artistic director of the American Repertory Theater. The Distinguished Alumni Award is given to Lily Afshar (B.M. '81, guitar).

June 2011: Yasuko "Yasi" Tokunaga retires after twenty-one years of leading the Dance Department. Cathy Young, a noted choreographer and teacher of jazz dance, is named as her successor.

December 2011: The Conservatory purchases 132 Ipswich Street for $5.1 million. The school announces the purchase in January 2012.

2012: The positions of associate dean and assistant dean are established.

2012: Chamber music is the latest addition to the Conservatory Connections offerings.

June 2012: Tony Award–winning director Michael Mayer and Obie Award–winning actor Alvin Epstein, who performed for a number of years with the American Repertory Theater, receive honorary degrees at the school's graduation. The Distinguished Alumni Award is given to Eugenia O'Brien Douglas (B.F.A. '73, dance).

2013: The Boston Conservatory becomes the first conservatory to present an Autism-Friendly Performance.

June 2013: American theater director Martha Clarke and renowned soprano Lucy Shelton receive honorary degrees at the Conservatory graduation ceremony, and the Distinguished Alumni Award is given to Anne Nathan (B.F.A. '85, musical theater).

2013: The school's dining services contract is transferred from Northeastern University to Berklee College of Music.

2013: Gender-neutral housing is offered to resident students.

2013–2014 academic year: The Boston Conservatory International Student Forum starts.

2014: The Conservatory launches its most ambitious capital campaign, *150th Anniversary Campaign: Exceeding Expectations*, which aims to raise $21 million. Funding will strengthen the Conservatory's endowment, provide much-needed funds for capital projects, and support the school's annual operating budget. The campaign concludes in conjunction with the school's 150th anniversary in 2017.

June 2014: Dwight Rhoden, choreographer and artistic director of Complexions Contemporary Ballet, receives an honorary degree at commencement, and the Distinguished Alumni Award is given to Russell DeVuyst (B.M. '78, trumpet), principal trumpet of Montreal Symphony.

June 2015: The Boston Conservatory and Berklee announce that they have signed a Memorandum of Understanding that allows the schools to formally explore the possibility of a merger.

June 2015: American pianist Gilbert Kalish and conductor and founder of Boston Musica Viva Richard Pittman receive honorary degrees. The Distinguished Alumni Award is given to Cynthia King (B.F.A. '77, dance).

September 2015: The Conservatory launches three new programs: B.F.A. in contemporary theater; B.F.A. in multidisciplinary stage management; and an M.M. in classical contemporary music performance.

November 2015: The social media hashtag #BoCoBackstage gains traction on the Instagram platform and quickly becomes a favorite way for student performers to communicate with the school's community and audience members with instantaneous "backstage" insight.

January 2016: The Boards of Trustees for The Boston Conservatory and Berklee College of Music, longtime neighbors in the Fenway neighborhood, announce the results of their separate votes regarding the merger: both boards unanimously approve to merge the two schools.

April 2016: *Backstage* magazine identifies the Conservatory's Dance Division as the top conservatory program in the country for contemporary dance.

2016: Dance Division Dean Cathy Young announces that the school has hired Duane Lee Holland, Jr. for the first joint hire between Berklee College of Music and the Conservatory,

and first full-time faculty position in hip-hop dance.

May 14, 2016: Dancer, choreographer, and director Debbie Allen delivers the commencement address, and superstar Broadway agent Joe Machota (M.M. '95, musical theater) is given the Distinguished Alumni Award. At the ceremony, at John Hancock Hall, the Conservatory confers degrees on 209 students, including 114 bachelor's degrees, 11 graduate performance diplomas, 79 master's degrees, 3 professional studies certificates, and 2 prestigious artist diplomas.

June 1, 2016: The Boston Conservatory completes the legal requirements to officially merge with Berklee. As part of the merger agreement, the school's name is changed to The Boston Conservatory at Berklee, later to be branded as Boston Conservatory at Berklee.

July 2016: The Conservatory debuts a new visual identity as a result of the merger with Berklee. The new visual identity includes a redesigned logo reflecting the Boston Conservatory at Berklee name, modified institutional colors, and a redesigned website using the URL, bostonconservatory.berklee.edu.

August 23, 2016: Boston Conservatory announces a historic partnership with the Royal Academy of Dance (RAD) in London that makes it the first performing arts institution in the United States to offer its students a RAD ballet teaching qualification.

November 2, 2016: Boston Conservatory announces its first joint program with Berklee, Boston Conservatory Opera Intensive at Valencia. The three-week summer program is designed and taught by Conservatory faculty for singers looking to pursue a career in opera. The program takes places at Berklee's campus in Valencia, Spain.

February 2017: The Conservatory hosts an internal celebration of its 150th anniversary.

May 2017: The Conservatory formally celebrates its 150th anniversary with a gala and special performance at Symphony Hall.

2016: Merger with Berklee

2016: Duane Lee Holland, Jr. hired

Afterword

Roger H. Brown, President of Berklee

The World I Live In

I have refused to live
locked in the orderly house of
⠀⠀⠀⠀⠀reasons and proofs.
The world I live in and believe in
is wider than that. And anyway,
⠀⠀⠀⠀⠀what's wrong with Maybe?

You wouldn't believe what once or
twice I have seen. I'll just
⠀⠀⠀⠀⠀tell you this:
only if there are angels in your head will
⠀⠀⠀⠀⠀you ever, possibly, see one.

By Mary Oliver

It's not often that the words "conservatory" and "progressive" are used in conjunction with one another, however the defining characteristic of Boston Conservatory's 150-year history is the progressive approach it has always brought to its arts education mission. Whether we consider that it was the first conservatory to enroll African American students, the fact that it launched a dance program that extended the tradition to focus on contemporary dance, that a major strength of the institution is an innovative program for autistic musicians, or that it was the first conservatory to recognize and create a musical theater major—time and again, Boston Conservatory has never been afraid of breaking down barriers.

Berklee has been fortunate to have a neighbor and peer institution at the leading edge of arts education. Since our foundings, Berklee and Boston Conservatory have been close partners—sharing dorm space, employing faculty who taught at both institutions, providing students with access to each other's classes through a consortium of local colleges, and jointly championing the founding of the Boston Arts Academy, Boston's first and only magnet high school for music, dance, theater, and visual arts. It was during one of our regular walks together that my friend and colleague Richard Ortner and I found ourselves asking, "What if?" What if we could combine our respective strengths to create the most comprehensive training ground for performing arts education?

And so the Conservatory has continued its progressive journey, passing through yet another doorway of reinvention, and emerging as Boston Conservatory at Berklee. I commend and respect the visionary leadership of Richard Ortner, who had the courage and commitment to bring our institutions together to forge an educational environment that will enable the next generation of performing artists and arts professionals to thrive and lead the field.

As our creative communities unite, there will be—and have already been—surprising and unexpected synergies. With music, movement, and digital technology converging, artists possess powerful new means of creative expression in the theater, on the concert stage, and through emerging platforms. This interplay of artists and modes of expression will position our institution as a leader in exploring new and original art forms, breaking down boundaries that isolate genres, and unleashing the tremendous creative potential of the global arts community.

Together, we will extend this progressive approach at the heart of the Conservatory to nurture the growth of the world's most inspired artists in music, theater, and dance so they may fully realize their creative and career potential. And in so doing we will give a voice to the angels in our heads and hearts.

January 2017

Photo Credits

Eric Antoniou, 111, 115, 126, 129, 145, 147, 151, 154, 167, 175, 177, 183

Bettmann, Getty Images Contributor, 48

Boston Conservatory at Berklee Archives, x, xi, 3, 5, 9, 16, 17, 18, 19, 20, 21, 25, 26, 29, 45, 47, 51, 53, 54, 62, 65, 67, 69, 70, 71, 75, 77, 79, 80, 87, 88, 91, 92, 97, 98, 101, 103, 105, 106, 108, 109, 111, 115, 117, 118, 124, 125, 126, 135, 143, 145, 165, 196

The Boston Globe Archives, 13, 22, 25, 91

Boston Public Library Archives, 5, 9

Boston Symphony Orchestra Archives, 39, 40

Chuck Choi, 69, 71, 165, 206

Jim Coleman, 171, 183

Cryptic C62, 113

Michael Cuscuna, Getty Images Contributor, 57

Courtesy of Dance Theatre of Harlem Archives, 91

Kelly Davidson, 143, 178, 206

Courtesy of Marti Epstein, 169

T. Charles Erickson for Boston Lyric Opera, 29

Jeremy Ayres Fischer, 185

Dave Green, 167

Courtesy of the E. Azalia Hackley Collection of African Americans in the Performing Arts, Detroit Public Library, 57, 59

Claudia Hansen, 169

Andreas Herbas, 191

Courtesy of Jonathon Bailey Holland, 169

Hiroyuki Ito, Getty Images Contributor, 33

Alex Irvin, 115

The Historic Images Outlet, 34

Jazz Legacy Label, 59

Julius Quartet, 9

Courtesy of Kate Ladenheim, 181

Library of Congress Prints and Photographs Division Washington, D.C., 23, 43

Liz Linder Photography, 118, 121, 147, 177, 192, 204

Joan Marcus, 129

Bruce Martin, 140

Courtesy of Steven McGraw, 83

Courtesy of Bob Monica, 83

Murphy Made Photography 2016, 129

Courtesy of Museum of Fine Arts, Boston, 189

Music Division, The New York Public Library. "[Ary Dulfer]" New York Public Library Digital Collections. Accessed March 13, 2017, 25

National Music Museum, University of South Dakota, 15

New York Daily News, 99, 101

Courtesy of Wang Meng Ngee, 157

David Nilsson for Boston Symphony Orchestra Archives, 40

Courtesy of Ryan O'Brien, 85

Courtesy of Bradley Pennington, 30

Gilles Petard, Getty Images, Contributor, 61, 65

Matthew Peyton, for Fox/Getty Images for Fox, 95

John Phelan, 113

The Priestley's Fine Art Photography, 106, 115, 123, 136

Courtesy of ProArts Consortium, 112

Courtesy of Marissa Rae Roberts, 172

Schlesinger Library, Radcliffe Institute, Harvard University, 9, 10, 43, 197

Schomburg Center for Research in Black Culture, Photographs and Prints Division, The New York Public Library. "P. G. Lowery's Band & Minstrels, part of the Ringling Bros. & Barnum & Bailey Circus." New York Public Library Digital Collections. Accessed March 13, 2017, 15

Richard Termine for Playbill.com, 129

Courtesy of Tommy Thompson, 111

Courtesy of Nate Tucker, 159

University of Nebraska-Lincoln Archives and Special Collections, 37

Videri String Quartet, 195

Liza Voll, 171

Max Wagenblass, 26, 75, 105, 113, 151, 152, 163, 167, 175, 195

Courtesy of Ebony Williams, 139

Courtesy of Gemma Williams, 177